Sue Phillips
9307 Ellen Dr
Highland, IN 46322-2926

P9-DDB-117

The Pampered Chef®

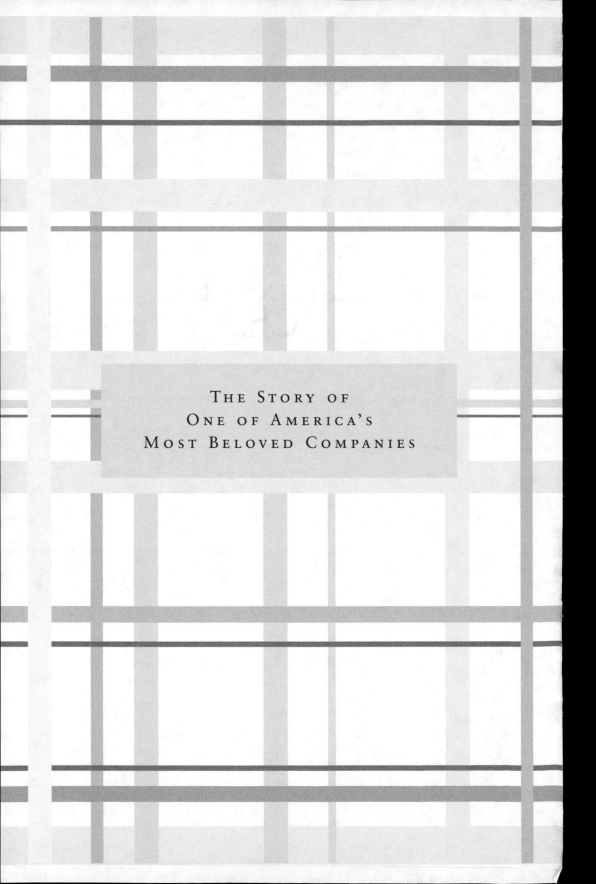

THE STORY OF
ONE OF AMERICA'S
MOST BELOVED COMPANIES

Doris Christopher

CURRENCY

DOUBLEDAY

New York   London   Toronto   Sydney   Auckland

A CURRENCY BOOK
PUBLISHED BY DOUBLEDAY
a division of Random House, Inc.

CURRENCY is a trademark of Random House, Inc., and DOUBLEDAY is
a registered trademark of Random House, Inc.

Library of Congress Cataloging-in-Publication Data is on file with the
Library of Congress
ISBN 0-385-51535-9

PRINTED IN THE UNITED STATES OF AMERICA

First Edition: July 2005

All trademarks are the property of their respective companies.

SPECIAL SALES
Currency Books are available at special discounts for bulk purchases
for sales promotions or premiums. Special editions, including
personalized covers, excerpts of existing books, and corporate imprints,
can be created in large quantities for special needs. For more
information, write to Special Markets, Currency Books,
specialmarkets@randomhouse.com

10   9   8   7   6   5   4   3   2   1

CONTENTS

*This book is dedicated to my husband, Jay,
whose commitment, support, love, and hard work
helped to create and build The Pampered Chef.
And, to our daughters, Julie and Kelley, who
were our inspiration to build a business that
celebrates families.*

In September of 2002, Doris Christopher, the founder of The Pampered Chef, came to see me in Omaha about selling the company. Right on the spot, I knew I wanted The Pampered Chef in the Berkshire Hathaway family. So we immediately made a deal.

The typical "entrance" strategy for acquisitions at Berkshire is to buy a company with great economic characteristics: no debt, a robust balance sheet, and positive cash flow. The Pampered Chef has all of that in spades. But it was Doris herself that cinched the deal for me. I liked her management style—hands-on, straightforward, nurturing, and accessible.

I also liked her reason for selling the company. There was no financial crisis, Doris had no health problems. She and her husband, Jay, simply wanted to plan for the future of their company to make sure it—and The Pampered Chef's Co-workers and Consultants—would continue to thrive long after Doris retired. That's the right way for an owner to behave, and therefore our "entrance" strategy made perfect sense to me. And that's important, because here at Berkshire, we have no "exit" strategy. We buy great businesses to keep. My job is to stay out of the way. And let Doris and her team run the business.

As you will read in this remarkable book, The Pampered Chef was founded in 1980 when Doris Christopher was a thirty-five-year-old suburban former home economics teacher with a husband and two little girls. Her initial goal was limited: she simply wanted to supplement her family's modest income. She had absolutely no business background. She turned to thinking about what she knew best—food preparation. Why not, she wondered, make a business out of marketing quality kitchenware, focusing on the items she herself had found most useful?

To launch her company, Doris borrowed $3,000 against a family life insurance policy—all the money *ever* injected into the company—and went to the Merchandise Mart in Chicago to buy the products she would offer for sale. She set up operations in her basement. Her plan was to conduct in-home presentations to small groups of women, gathered at the homes of their friends. While driving to her first presentation, Doris almost talked herself into returning home, convinced she was doomed to fail. But the women to whom she demonstrated her wares that evening loved her, and The Pampered Chef was under way. Working with her husband, Jay, Doris did $50,000 of business in the first year.

Today—the twenty-fifth anniversary of the company—The Pampered Chef has thousands of Kitchen Consultants, serving 12 million customers at one million Kitchen Shows a year.

I saw this business for myself when I attended my first Kitchen Show. I put on my Pampered Chef apron and chopped, tasted, and tested right along with the other guests. I wasn't a star, however, coming in last in the apple-peeling contest. It was easy to see why the business is a success. The company's products, in large part proprietary, are well designed, finely crafted, and, above all, useful, and the Pampered Chef Consultants are knowledgeable and enthusiastic.

The Pampered Chef is truly loved by its customers because it has found a need and filled it exceptionally well, helping every-day home cooks to become masters of their own home kitchens and making mealtime preparation quick, easy, and fun. It also offers its Consultants an incomparable business opportunity, al-lowing men and women to build a home-based business of their own, based on Doris Christopher's personal blueprint for suc-cess. When you read the profiles of The Pampered Chef's Kitchen Consultants in Chapter 8, you may wonder what you're doing in your nine-to-five cubicle while these folks are happily cooking their way to fame and fortune.

At Berkshire Hathaway, we like companies that are easy to understand. Doris Christopher's "keep it simple" approach has a lot to teach anyone who is reaching for the American Dream. Frankly, if I can't understand a company's business, I figure their customers must have a pretty hard time figuring it out, too.

I would challenge anyone on Wall Street to take $3,000 and do what Doris Christopher has done: build a business from scratch into a world-class organization. But follow the simple steps in this book, and it just might happen. Come see me in Omaha when you've put together your own recipe for success; we pay cash and Berkshire's check will clear. In the meantime, read this book. Then, read it again.

—Warren Buffett

INTRODUCTION

I've read about people who claim they had a complete vision of the success of their business at the very start. I confess that in 1980 when I started The Pampered Chef, I could not even imagine the company we are today. I had no vision of grandeur. I just wanted to make enough money to contribute to our household income and the future college education of our two young daughters.

After eight years as a stay-at-home mom with my two preschool daughters, I was anxious to reenter the workforce. A former home economist and teacher, I wanted to draw upon my past experience, but coming up with what to do was difficult. Because Julie and Kelley were eight and five, I was looking for something with flexible hours that would allow me to be at home for them after school. I always placed family before career then, as I do now. I soon found that this priority eliminated a lot of jobs.

The only thing left was to start my own company! From my

days as a home economist, I knew a great deal about quality kitchen tools, which, at that time, were hard to find in retail stores. And since the high point of our day as a family often took place as we gathered around the supper table, I soon knew what my goal was to be. Our company's purpose, products, and marketing efforts would focus on a mission uniquely ours: bringing families together at the table for shared mealtimes, and quality kitchen tools would help them do just that!

When I first went into business, it was a one-woman operation. My four-hundred-square-foot combination office–storage area was the unfinished basement of our modest frame home in the Chicago suburb of River Forest. I financed it with $3,000 I borrowed from an insurance policy on my husband Jay's life. From this humble beginning, I embarked on a career of selling kitchen tools to small groups of women in their homes. In the evenings after Jay and I had dinner with our children, I conducted "Kitchen Shows." During the day, while Julie and Kelley were in school, I selected, purchased, stored, and managed my inventory. There was also bookkeeping, processing, packaging, delivering—whatever had to be done, I did it. In my one-woman show, I did everything from answering the phone to emptying wastepaper baskets.

This was not particularly unusual. The responsibilities I had as a start-up entrepreneur are par for the course for the millions of Americans who launch small businesses. It consumes as much time as a fledgling entrepreneur is willing to give it. However, being there for my family always came first, so I had to perform a real juggling act to manage our household and in between take care of business. I was blessed with a supportive husband who shared my enthusiasm for my work—Jay was also my mentor, adviser, and cheerleader. He willingly pitched in with everything ranging from child care to bookkeeping. Without his support, I don't see how my tiny business would have ever got off the ground. We all need other people to succeed at anything we do, and boy, did I ever need Jay!

Throughout this book, I'll give you a step-by-step description of how The Pampered Chef survived the initial stages of a neophyte company and went on to thrive as an organization that today occupies a 780,000-square-foot facility. We now have a thousand Co-workers who do what I did as a sole proprietor, but of course on a much larger scale—and with the systems we now have in place, in a much more sophisticated way. Note too that there are 70,000 independent "Kitchen Consultants" who annually conduct one million Kitchen Shows for twelve million Pampered Chef customers. These women and men share my dedication to providing expert advice and inspiration to millions of people who yearn to make mealtime truly family time.

Looking back to when I was the one and only Kitchen Consultant, I am in awe at all that has happened since. Quite obviously, what the company has accomplished is a result of the labor of many. I am blessed to work with a talented team of dedicated people. Were it not for the combined efforts of many, starting with our Kitchen Consultants, I'd still be working out of the basement of our home in River Forest.

In preparation for writing this book, I have given considerable thought to the amazing journey Jay and I have traveled. This exercise required serious soul searching, and it forced me to recall many personal events in my life that contributed to the creation of The Pampered Chef. Some of these incidents were temporary setbacks that turned out to be blessings in disguise. Others were so remote they seemed insignificant at the time but later proved to be crucial. In retrospect, it is as if each incident was a small piece of a large puzzle. And remember: it only takes one missing piece to render a puzzle incomplete.

As you read my story, I will reveal each of these magic moments in detail and explain their implication. I view life as an ongoing adventure in which many things happen along the way that seem unimportant but later prove essential in reaching one's destination. Such things have repeatedly happened to me, some of which at the time made no sense whatsoever. It would be easy to write them off as fate; however, I choose to give credit where it is due. I believe it has been God's hand at work. He has been instrumental in guiding me and the result has been an enterprise that serves tens of thousands of Pampered Chef people, whose work, in turn, enriches millions of families by bringing them together at mealtime. Along the way, we have been blessed to be able to give back by embracing such causes as hunger relief, early breast cancer detection, and family resiliency. The joy of giving is the gift from God that I cherish most.

In recent years we began to realize the importance of having a succession plan in place so that The Pampered Chef could prosper long after I would no longer be with the company. In 2004, The Pampered Chef became part of Warren Buffett's Berkshire Hathaway Company. We chose to take this route at a time when the company was strong and healthy, well in advance of my retirement as CEO and chairman. I didn't want to be one of those company founders who thought he or she was indispensable and had no one in line to take the reins in the event of disability or untimely demise. This company and my associates mean too much to me to allow my ego to get in the way.

Meanwhile, it was quite a compliment to join Berkshire Hathaway, listed by *Fortune* in 2004 as the nation's second most admired company. I am honored that Warren Buffett, one of the world's most respected and astute businessmen, thinks that highly of our company.

So this book is about a company with roots tracing back to

a modest beginning in the basement of our home, and how it went on to become a member of one of the world's most prestigious businesses. Let me tell you, it's been quite a ride. And the journey continues, because it doesn't have a final destination. It is indeed ongoing and never-ending.

My story begins with my life as a young girl growing up in the rural community of Oak Lawn, near Chicago. I have been described as the typical girl next door, and although I was a conscientious, above-average student, I never stood out in a crowd—not then or now. This is why I believe what happened to me can happen to you. I invite you to come with me as I tell my story—our story. May it furnish you with inspiration to take a wonderful journey of your own.

I

SMALL-TOWN GIRL
FROM CHICAGO

As a little girl, on our family trips to Michigan, I'd tell everyone I was from Chicago. But the truth is, I grew up in Oak Lawn, Illinois, twelve miles southwest of the Loop. We were definitely not big-city folk. Oak Lawn was a small, rural community, away from the hustle and bustle of life in the metropolis.

Growing up in the 1950s and '60s, my two older sisters and I were raised with old-fashioned, small-town values. Our family knew our neighbors on both sides of the street. Few families bothered to lock their doors. We didn't watch much television and there weren't any VCRs, CDs, or video games. Instead, my friends and I cut out paper dolls and played hide-and-seek in the backyard. On Saturday night I'd sometimes gather around the dining room table with my family or friends to play tripoly.

Oak Lawn was an unincorporated rural area, so there wasn't a lot there. The subdivision where we lived was a lower-middle-class neighborhood with no sidewalks. Our small Cape Cod house, 8605 South Seventy-eighth Court, was a mile or so from Harlem

Avenue, a main thoroughfare in Chicago that runs north and south for some fifty miles. While houses on our street were inexpensive, they were well maintained. The residents took pride in their front lawns: grass was regularly mowed, hedges were tidily trimmed, and flowerbeds were neatly manicured into decorative rows.

Some families spent a lot of time on their small front porches on hot evenings. Although we didn't use our porch as a gathering place, it had an awning and a couple of chairs. As a small child, I played games on that porch, but it saw its best use as a site for picture-taking sessions on important occasions. Our family albums are filled with photographs of my two sisters and me on the porch, starting with our baby pictures. Later we appear there dressed in our Easter outfits, confirmation dresses, prom dresses, and of course our graduation robes.

Back then, there were no nearby supermarkets. My folks did their grocery shopping several miles away at the Jewel Tea store. When I was in high school, a Pic & Save Super Market was built on what had been an empty lot. Its grand opening was a major event in our community. We had finally arrived! "It's one of those Pic & Saves just like they have in Chicago," my mother said, her voice ringing with pride.

There weren't any self-service gasoline stations, either. Ted Kelley, my father, owned and operated a one-man service station, a relic of the past. Cities Service Station, located in Logan Square, a community on the North Side of Chicago, was open from seven to seven, six days a week. Daddy left home around six in the morning and returned around eight at night, so during the week we didn't get to spend a lot of time with him. A hardworking man, he pumped gas and checked everything under the hood—the oil, the water, the batteries. He always cleaned the windshield, even when it wasn't dirty. A top-rate mechanic, my father also repaired cars.

Daddy was bushed when he walked in the door each night. His hands were so filthy from oil and grease, he'd scrub his fingernails for ten minutes before sitting down at the dinner table. My sisters and I were too hungry to wait for Daddy's arrival, so my mother prepared an early dinner for the four of us and a later meal for my father. An extremely organized woman, Mother devised a unique dinner system. One night she cooked for us and reheated leftovers for my father. The next night she served us leftovers and prepared a fresh dinner for Dad. Mother rotated who got the fresh dinner: Daddy, then us, his turn, our turn. And oh yes, my father's older brother, Bernard—Uncle Bun to us—was a regular guest for a good home-cooked meal, at least three times during the week and most Sundays.

Once I was out of kindergarten, my mother went back to her old job as a typist in the claims department of an insurance company. Prior to that, she worked part time, around my schedule. A hard worker like my father, my mother worked full time during her career for several insurance companies, all located in downtown Chicago. Jane Kelley was ahead of her time. In those days, most households had only one wage earner. Women customarily stopped working outside the home once they had children. My mother, however, was an excellent typist, and seeing how hard my father worked, she wanted to bring in some supplemental income so he'd someday be able to slow down. Although I never felt the slightest bit in need, looking back today I know that my parents had to struggle to make ends meet. Just the same, I was always proud of the fact that my father was a self-employed businessman.

Being his own boss was important to my father. It meant nobody could give him orders and no one could ever fire him. In truth, the big oil companies drew up one-sided contracts with their independent operators that actually took away their independence. But my sisters and I didn't know that. In our eyes, Ted Kelley stood tall. He was his own man. And most importantly, he was a good man. In my eyes, he was the best.

SUNDAY—MY FAVORITE DAY OF THE WEEK

In the Kelley house, the highlight of the week was our family Sunday dinner after the church service. This made Sunday my favorite day of the week. We were together as a family. Daddy took on an entirely different appearance on Sunday. He enjoyed dressing up for church: he'd put on a freshly pressed suit, always with a starched white shirt and a stylish tie. He seemed to feel so much better about himself than when he wore his gas station uniform. I loved seeing him in his Sunday clothes. He looked so handsome I thought he could have passed for a bank president. St. Paul's Lutheran Church was at the end of the block on Seventy-eighth Court, and I'd be all smiles as I walked there with my father. The one-room wood-frame church had a capacity of fifty, too small for a full-time pastor, so a visiting pastor conducted the service. The building was so tiny that when Sunday school classes were conducted prior to the service, volunteer teachers assembled the children into small classes, each grade occupying a separate pew.

Sunday was my mother's favorite day, too. A superb cook, Mama stayed behind in her favorite place, the kitchen. After spending a good portion of the morning making our Sunday supper, she always arrived just in time for the service. Everyone in the tiny church knew when Mother walked in because she often smelled of fried chicken.

We'd be sitting in our pew, and without turning, my oldest sister Barbara would nudge my sister Donna and whisper, "Take a whiff. Mama's here."

"Why does she always have to make fried chicken?" Donna lamented. "Why can't she cook something nobody could smell?"

I thought she smelled delicious, but my sisters were old enough to be embarrassed by it. In my mind, Mama was the best cook in our neighborhood, and that was something to be proud of, certainly not an embarrassment.

On school nights my sisters and I would rush through dinner, help clean up, then hit the books. My mother would then reset the table for my father. On Sundays, however, we ate leisurely. We generally wore our church clothes at the table, the one meal of the week where we'd be together as a family unit. Dinner conversations ran the gamut from church activities to current events. My father's divorced older brother, Bernard, was a regular Sunday guest. Uncle Bun and Daddy were sports enthusiasts, and after dinner they'd talk baseball, football, hockey—whatever was in season. With four females in the house, when Uncle Bun wasn't there, dinner conversations were more girl talk. My father, a very quiet, soft-spoken man, could hardly get a word in edgewise.

When I think back to my youth, some of my most pleasant memories are those dinners on Sunday and holidays when the whole family gathered around the table. At Thanksgiving, one of my mother's brothers and his family came to stay with us. One of Mama's sisters and her family visited during Christmas holidays. These enjoyable family times around the dinner table were an inspiration to my career, because the coming together at the dinner table became the central theme of The Pampered Chef.

BACK AND FORTH TO SCHOOL

Wanting me to have a good Christian education, my parents enrolled me in Zion Lutheran Grade School. They felt that I would get more individual attention at a school with small classes. My two older sisters went to the local public grade school. They couldn't have gone to Zion Lutheran because we had limited transportation at our house. My mother didn't drive, so she had to leave the house with my father at six every morning and he'd drop her off at the train station on his way to work. Zion Lutheran was in Summit, a town ten miles away, and in the same direction as my sister Donna's high school. Early each morning, Donna and I walked to the bus stop. We rode the bus together until Donna got off at the Argo High School stop, seven blocks from Zion, where I got off. Had it not been for my sister, I would have attended the local public grade school because I was too young to take the bus alone.

Coming home from school was another story. Uncle Bun worked in a factory in the area, and my mother would take a bus from downtown Chicago to Argo, where Uncle Bun picked up the two of us at 5:00 p.m. This meant I had more than an hour to kill after school. It was only a ten-minute walk from school to Argo, so I had to dilly-dally around until my rendezvous with Mama and Uncle Bun.

Sometimes I'd go to a girlfriend's house, Gail's or Eileen's, but mostly I'd hang out with one or both of them at the drugstore or candy shop. With all the time I had to kill, their parents probably thought I was a bad influence on their daughters. Remember, back then, it was unusual for a mother to work full time like mine, although Gail's and Eileen's mothers did have part-time jobs. No matter how much free time I had after school, I always had to meet my mother and Uncle Bun at the bus stop at

5:00. It seemed that my entire day revolved around my transportation to and from school.

When I finished eighth grade, it was decided that I should continue my education at Walther Lutheran High School, a private school in Melrose Park. My mother placed a high value on education, as did her mother.

MEETING JAY

More often than not, the school bus arrived at Walther late, after the first-period bell. I was embarrassed whenever I had to walk into the middle of a class in session. But one time it worked to my advantage in a big way. During my freshman year, my locker was across the hall from Jay Christopher's first-period class. The classroom had a door with a glass window and Jay could see me at my locker from his desk, hurriedly throwing my coat and books into the locker, gathering up whatever I needed.

Jay used to watch me come and go, and because the lockers were assigned alphabetically to students, mine was right next to his basketball teammate Tom Klammer's. "Who's the cute girl with her locker next to yours?" Jay asked Tom one day. "You know, the one who's always late getting to school."

Shortly after I started my sophomore year, Jay surprised me by asking me to be his date for the school's homecoming dance. Poor Jay didn't know it, but nobody at Walther lived farther away than I did. So that Saturday morning, he drove all the way out to my house to pick me up for a parade and a football game. As we continued to date, I'm sure his parents wondered why Jay couldn't have found a girl who lived closer.

TYPING CLASS — MY WATERLOO

An honor student, I wasn't worried when I began typing class in my junior year at Walther. My mother typed for a living, so I figured I had the genes for it. It would be a breeze. One of the easier courses, it would be useful in college for typing essays and reports. Jay had taken typing the previous year, and he was already using his skills to fill out college applications.

Mrs. Stryker, an elderly woman whom I'd had for World History, taught typing. She was a gruff lady with a no-nonsense attitude. The first day in typing class, she said, "I am going to assign a character to each of you. One of you will be a snail, another a rabbit, a dolphin, a breed of dog, a cat, and so on. Every day, your designated character will appear on the bulletin board. As you progress from one typing lesson to the next, your animal will move forward. Your advancement will be tracked. Naturally, some of you will advance at a faster rate than others, but at the end of the semester, hopefully everyone's character will end up at the finish line. And when this happens, you will be an able typist."

Characters were handed out, and mine was a turtle. Better a turtle than a snail, I thought to myself.

"Now remember, class," Mrs. Stryker said, "although your progress will be tracked, you're not competing against each other. This is just a way to make the class a little more interesting."

Right from the beginning, everyone else in the class appeared to catch on, but I couldn't make heads or tails out of Mrs. Stryker's instructions. As each day passed I became more confused. Maybe my hand-eye coordination was not particularly good. Whatever it was, I was totally lost.

Mrs. Stryker played music so that we could type to it, to give us a rhythm. Everyone caught on quickly except me. I found the music distracting. It only added to my frustration and confusion.

My turtle was in last place. At first it was only slightly behind the other characters, then it fell more behind the pack. Soon the gap between the rest of the animals and my turtle seemed vast.

I had always been successful in school. But now I was far and away the worst student in typing class. Not only was I slow, I made so many errors that even when my turtle advanced past the starting line, my errors would move it back again. I languished at zero. With my typing errors, I was actually less than zero, but Mrs. Stryker kindly never moved my turtle behind the starting line.

This went on for several weeks. When I walked into typing class, I was tense and nervous, and the feeling of humiliation lasted all day long. One day Mrs. Stryker took me aside. "Doris, you did so well in my world history class. I expect much more from you in this class."

At home, I told my parents about my predicament. "I'm absolutely the worst in my class. Maybe even the worst in the history of the school."

"You've got to learn how to type," my mother said. "Even if you don't go into secretarial work, typing will be useful all of your life. Just hang in there, honey! I'm sure something will click and you'll catch up with the other kids. I know you can do it."

Mama even gave me typing tips at the dinner table, but it didn't matter. Each day, the class kept getting worse. It's not going to work, I kept thinking.

"My fingers keep hitting the wrong keys," I pleaded to her.

When my mother saw how miserable it was making me, she made a suggestion. "If it's not too late, try replacing typing with something else. You can retake typing during your senior year. Meanwhile, I'll work with you on it."

My two older sisters were not pleased. "Why are you letting her drop a course?" Barbara asked. "You never let us!"

I checked out my options and found a home economics class I could take to replace typing.

I had never considered the home ec course before because I was taking college preparatory classes. I didn't think I had time for home ec. But now, this was my way out. I'll just take it during my junior year, I told myself.

So, with my mother's support, I made the switch. As it turned out, the home economics course was a piece of cake for me. I took to it like a duck to water, and enrolled in both my junior and senior years.

As I look back, had I been a better typist, I would never have taken the home economics course. And had I not taken it, I am certain I would never have started The Pampered Chef. It's a case of trusting that when one door closes, God opens a window for us somewhere else.

FEAR OF SPEAKING

Today I address several thousand people at our Pampered Chef conferences. People assume that speaking in front of an audience comes naturally to me. In fact, for years I had a strong fear of speaking that probably stems from my teenage years when I watched my father stand up to speak in front of our small congregation in church. Ted Kelley was a faithful servant and a hard church worker, but when it came time for him to speak out on an issue he felt passionate about, he would just choke up. It was hard for me to watch my father, unable to get the words out of his mouth. He was a quiet, shy man. But, to me, his youngest daughter, he was the pillar of strength. If he was so afraid to speak, how could I think about addressing an audience? For years after, I did my best to avoid speaking in front of a group.

There was a required speaking course for all Walther students who planned to attend college. Throughout my high school career, I shuddered at the thought that someday I would have to take that course. Curiously, while I despised public speaking, I had no problem acting in school plays. Acting was different—in a controlled setting, I had lines to perform in someone else's character. In fact, I won the lead role in my junior class play, a musical called *Smiling Through,* as well as the lead role in our senior class play, *Ask Any Girl.* But I was terrified of speaking in public. My senior year, I finagled my way out of taking that dreaded speech course because it conflicted with a home economics class I was taking. And by this time, my mind was made up: I wanted to be a home economics major in college.

"The home economics course is so important to me," I pleaded with a school official. "Besides, I'll never have to make a speech in my entire life. Can't I get credit for speech class through my participation in school plays?"

My pleading worked. Later, at the University of Illinois, the school had a speech requirement for anyone graduating with a teaching degree; I purposely took a course in voice and diction because it didn't involve speaking in front of an audience. Years later, when it became apparent that my work would involve speaking in front of audiences, I regretted missing out on those public speaking courses.

MOTHER'S SUPPORT

My sisters and I could always count on my mother to be in our corner—always. She was not a pushover. Far from it. With that typing class, in the beginning, she and my big sisters were dead set against me dropping the course. But in the end, my mother realized how much it was upsetting me and she fully supported my decision to substitute home economics for typing. "I know you don't agree with me," she told Barbara and Donna. "But Doris is dropping typing. She has my consent so there will be no more discussion on the subject."

It was my mother who ran the house. I don't mean to imply that my father was oblivious to us, but his work was so demanding, he just wasn't home enough to get involved in our activities. Mama wasn't the domineering type and actually had a soft personality. She was, however, strong-willed when it came to doing what she believed was right for her family.

For example, my sister Donna was an excellent student but she tested poorly on standardized tests. As a result of her low science and math scores, she was accepted to nursing school conditionally. My mother wasn't about to take this sitting down. She contacted the nursing schools where Donna applied and explained that sometimes an outstanding student tests poorly, but the results are not indicative of how the student will fare in his or her studies. She persuaded the school to let Donna take a series of interviews. Ultimately Donna was fully accepted and excelled in nursing school.

During my senior year at Walther, I applied to the University of Illinois, known for its excellent home economics department. A lot of people told me to go to a smaller school. "The Champaign campus has twenty thousand students," I was warned. "You'll be just a number there." Others said, "You're used to this little high school of five hundred students where you get a lot of attention. Don't go there, Doris!"

My uncle Dave, a social worker in Michigan, was the person Mama relied on the most for academic advice. Uncle Dave insisted that I should not go to the University of Illinois. "Doris will be lost there," he said firmly.

"Thank you for your advice, Dave, but this is what Doris wants to do, and do you know what? I think she can do it. So that's where she's going to college."

That was my mother. Whatever we truly wanted to do, she was for—and she would never stand in our way. My parents scraped and saved to send me to college. But if I wanted to go to Illinois, she was behind me 100 percent, despite the financial burden. Later, when I told her that I was having some problems in a college math course, she calmly said, "Okay, Doris, you have to get a tutor."

With my mother, it was always "This is what we're going to do." There was never an obstacle that couldn't be overcome. To her, every barrier was only a temporary roadblock. There was always a solution. Even if she opposed something, she would work with us to find a solution. "Okay, Doris, if you want this, I'm going to help you figure out a way to get it."

Years after I graduated from college, I invited my mother to come with me to a Kitchen Show, as I eventually came to call them. She had always been supportive of everything I did, but I could tell by her lack of interest that she wasn't excited about my business. Although she was too gracious to say anything negative, some of her remarks suggested that she wondered why I wanted to be in direct sales when I had majored in home economics and had had some teaching experience. By this time, my father had passed away and she had relocated to Kalamazoo to be near her two remaining sisters.

I wanted my mother to see what I actually did at a Kitchen Show. I probably could have picked a better one for her to attend—because we had to climb three flights of stairs in an apartment building to conduct this one. To top it off, the family had a big Doberman pinscher that scared us half to death. And where did he sit? You guessed it—right next to my mother. He looked as big as she did. But she just sat there and calmly petted it. She was in complete control and as cool as a cucumber. The sales from that evening's show were excellent and my mother seemed to enjoy it.

When we left, she said to me, "Doris, I'm so glad you invited me to that meeting. It was such a pleasure to see you speak to those people. You did such a good job in making those products come alive. And I was impressed with how much they bought. I'm so proud of you."

COLLEGE AND BEYOND

When I arrived on the Illinois campus, I understood why Uncle Dave said I'd be lost in such a big place. For the first time in my life I was away from home on my own and I was homesick. But that was part of the college experience, and a good one at that.

Jay was in his sophomore year at Valparaiso, a small, private liberal arts college in Valparaiso, Indiana. During my senior year of high school, Jay and I had been separated and we had both agreed we should date other people. So being far away from him was not a new adjustment. We had also agreed to date other people while we were in college. By dating others, neither of us would be stuck in a dormitory every weekend without a social life. Seeing other people would also make us more independent. If our love was true love, we reasoned, dating would make us appreciate each other all the more. We still saw each other, especially in the summertime when we were both home. Jay had a car and visited me throughout my four years in college, and I went to Valparaiso to see him, staying either with his aunt and uncle, who lived there, or with one of my high school girlfriends who went to school there.

As big as the university was, my home economics courses were confined to a small part of the campus. It was as if I were attending a small school within a big school. Once I realized this, I was no longer overwhelmed by its sheer size.

When I read the home economics curriculum, I felt like a little kid in a candy store, not knowing what to eat first. The core curriculum offered about thirty courses to home economics majors, and when I looked at it, I didn't know what to study first. In addition to courses in my major, I took the usual ones in everything from English to history. I had to work especially hard in microbiology, physiology, and organic chemistry because my science and math skills weren't strong. But in home economics I earned good grades in every course.

One of my favorite college courses was home management, where eight home economics seniors lived in the same residence for eight weeks, managing the house. Each girl had a specific responsibility for one week, and we took turns preparing meals, cleaning house, arranging hospitality, and managing the budget. We worked as a team within the house. I particularly loved the hospitality part: place settings, table decorations, floral arrangements, and entertaining. Some weeks the house had an austere budget and we had to be more budget-conscious in what we ate and to cut back on our entertainment expenses. The experience summed up what we had learned during our four years as home economic majors, and offered a great lesson in teamwork.

Like the seven other girls, I took the home management

course during the last semester in my senior year, and I also did my student teaching. I was sent to a high school in Joliet and taught sewing to a class of inner-city twelfth graders—five girls and two boys. I was twenty-one years old, and looked younger than several of my students. The kids were very cooperative. At the end of the semester, each student was required to sew a garment. The girls sewed a simple sleeveless shirt, but the boys had to put in sleeves, because guys didn't wear sleeveless shirts in the 1960s. Surprisingly, each boy made a shirt that not only earned him a passing grade but that he could wear proudly.

Jay graduated in June 1967 and I in August. After graduation, we were married, the beginning of an incredible journey together.

MY TEACHING YEARS

As newlyweds, we lived in Valparaiso, where Jay planned to enroll in law school and afterward practice with his father, who had a one-man office. Jay enrolled in John Marshall Law School in Chicago. I took a job in Chesterton, Indiana, teaching home economics to junior high and high school students at Liberty Township High School. Traveling back and forth to Chicago by train to attend John Marshall Law School, Jay decided, after six weeks, that law school was not what he wanted. So he got a job as a market research analyst with Hammond Organ Company, headquartered in Chicago. After my first year of teaching school, we moved to the Chicago area. It was already the beginning of August and, to my chagrin, all the teaching jobs I applied for had been filled. I called the placement office at the University of Illinois, and they discovered DuPage County was looking for a home economist for its Cooperative Extension Service, operated by the University of Illinois. I would be teaching home economics to adults in suburban and rural areas. The program served as an educational resource to people throughout the entire county, offering courses in home-related basics like nutrition, cooking, child care, family relations, family finances, home decorating, and so on. There were three home economists. We'd plan the lesson together, then we'd head out in different directions of the county to teach. Instead of having regular classrooms, we met in community centers, schools, libraries, banks, and private homes. I had my own office, but I spent most of my time in the field, traveling around rural areas of the county. Unlike teaching, where I had several lessons to prepare each day for the same students throughout the semester, with the extension program I'd give the same presentation ten to twenty times to different audiences at different locations. I liked being able to work on a presentation and get better at delivering it. While I enjoyed being a schoolteacher, this was a job I absolutely loved. I enjoyed having an office with my own desk, a phone, and a secretary. And I liked the traveling— meeting people from different areas of the county. It was a pleasure to work with adult students who were eager to learn. They were in class because they wanted to be. High school students did not always share the same desire. Typically, fifteen to thirty people attended each class, and before long I no longer had a fear of speaking—at least in this situation. Because we administered the county's 4H program, we also worked at the County Fair, conducting classes. I did this for six years, right up until a month before my first daughter, Julie, was born. That's when I took on a new job—as a full-time mom.

A FULL-TIME MOM

Julie was born May 21, 1972. We were living in Elmhurst, and through our church I met a lot of other young moms. Jay and I were a one-car family, but one of my girlfriends would always pick me up to go to a Bible class, play racquetball, grocery-shop, and so on. We'd bundle up our kids and take them along, whether it was a church activity or a walk in the park. Later, we'd get together at one of our houses for lunch. It was a wonderful time, and Jay and I developed many lifelong friendships.

In the meantime, Jay had left the Hammond Organ Company and worked for a while for Keebler, the cookie company, as director of operations. Then he took a job with the Lien Chemical Company, a privately held franchiser in the contract cleaning business. Lien's primary business was providing janitorial service to clean the restrooms at restaurants, gas stations, and bus terminals. It also offered full-service cleaning for large commercial buildings. It was a highly competitive, tough-sell business, and Jay had to be an innovative marketer to succeed at it. In retrospect, his experience with Lien contributed more to the businessperson he is today than any other job.

Three years later, we were blessed with another beautiful daughter. We took my maiden name and christened her Kelley. Taking care of an infant and a three-year-old was truly a full-time job; until I did it, I never realized how much work it was. I marvel at stay-at-home moms who have a house filled with young children. So no sooner had I stopped changing Julie's diapers than I was changing them again for Kelley—and enjoying early motherhood for the second time. Soon Julie was in school and I was participating in school activities, such as being a room mother and a picture lady. I was always one of the first mothers to volunteer to accompany Julie's class on field trips. I took great satisfaction in knowing I could fulfill my responsibility as a parent. Thinking back to my own childhood, this was missing in my mother's life. Since she always worked full time, she didn't have the option to be a volunteer.

Once Julie was in school, I thought about the day when I might return to the workforce. Strictly from a financial viewpoint, I knew I couldn't remain a stay-at-home mom forever. It was just a matter of time before I'd have to supplement our family income so we could assure that Julie and Kelley would receive a good college education. To make some extra money that we could put away for a nest egg for the girls, I worked at several part-time jobs. I taught sewing at Montgomery Ward in a one-hour class on Saturday mornings. Then I took in alterations. For a short while, I even did market research for a company that tested cake mixes.

One of the more interesting part-time jobs I did was to demonstrate Jenn-Air ranges, again a market research job. Here too I was hired because I was a home economist. In this job I worked at major appliance stores and at open houses conducted by kitchen design companies, demonstrating the ranges for four to five hours. While I enjoyed it, I was on call at their whim, and a lot of Saturday demonstrations took me away from my family. So I kept reading the classifieds, looking for my ideal job, a job where I could work part time around my family doing work that I enjoyed. There's got to be something out there, I kept telling myself.

REENTERING THE WORKFORCE

By the summer of 1980, I was thirty-five years old and I had been out of the workforce for eight years. Come September, both Julie and Kelley would be in school, and I started thinking about returning to full-time work. Raising my own children made me appreciate how truly remarkable my mother was. I marveled at the healthy balance she maintained between our home life and her career. While I loved being a stay-at-home mom, it was now time to move on.

Jay's career was rapidly progressing; however, I wanted to do my share. Jay and I realized that by the time our girls graduated from high school, it would take a small fortune to give them a college education. We knew we needed to start saving now. That gave me my goal. The money I made would also help pay for music lessons, summer camp, and other extras we wanted them to have. I didn't start out wanting to set the world on fire. I just wanted to find something to supplement our family income—extra money we could sock away for the future. Money I could earn to be put away for their education would allow them options for their future.

HAVING PRIORITIES

I asked Jay if he had any ideas about what kind of work I could do.

"Why don't we talk about what you *don't* want?" Jay suggested.

"That's easy," I answered. "I don't want to forgo being a full-time mom to the girls."

"Which means?"

"I want a job with flexible hours, so I can get them ready for school in the morning, see them off to school, and be here for them when they come home from school. I also want to be able to participate in their activities."

"Which means?"

"I want to be there when Julie and Kelley need me. And I don't want to miss a thing—not the first tooth, not a first ride on a two-wheeler. I don't want to miss any precious moments of their childhood that happen only once. I want to be a room mother, be able to volunteer to go on field trips, and later on, I know I'll want to be a Girl Scout leader. When they're sick, I want to stay at home and take care of them. I want to bake cookies with the girls after school. I want to take them to the library, the zoo, and those kinds of things. Isn't this what you want, Jay? We want to make sure we bring up our girls the right way."

"Of course," Jay said. "At the same time, you want to make some extra money. But you want to do it on your own terms."

"Exactly."

"Anything else you don't want to do?" Jay questioned.

"No work on weekends and especially on holidays," I added. "That's prime family time."

Jay shook his head. "One thing's for sure, you're not looking for a nine-to-five job. I'll say this, Doris, with your requirements, no one's going to hire you. I wouldn't hire you. You want to work but you don't want to work. Nobody gets hired on those kind of terms."

"I suppose I wouldn't hire me either."

Jay contemplated what I said. "Doris, if you're going to make those demands, you better start your own business, so you can be your own boss."

TAKING A SELF-INVENTORY

For weeks, it seemed like the only thing Jay and I talked about when we were alone was what I should do. Jay saw how frustrated I was, and he willingly listened and offered suggestions.

One evening after the girls had gone to bed, Jay carried a legal pad into the kitchen just as I was putting away the last dish. He said, "Doris, let's sit down and make a list of your skills and the things you like to do."

As we sat at the kitchen table, I said, "Put down cooking." After a while I added, "I love sewing. I also like teaching people. And I love to entertain people in our home."

"That's a great start, dear," he replied. "What jobs are there where you can do those kinds of things?"

"I don't see myself working for someone who owns a restaurant, but I could open one of my own."

Jay divided a page in half by drawing a line down the middle. At the top of the left side he wrote ADVANTAGES in big print, and on the right side, DISADVANTAGES.

"Okay, Doris, let's review the kinds of jobs you might consider, and for each one, we'll list what you like and dislike about it. Now before we begin, let's be realistic. There are disadvantages in every job. There is no such thing as the perfect job. We're trying to come up with a job that has the most pluses compared to its minuses. Or if there is a particular minus you can't live with, we will automatically eliminate that job.

"So, what are the advantages of owning a restaurant?" he asked.

"I'm my own boss," I answered. He wrote down "Own boss" on the left-hand side of the page.

"I love cooking. I'm a people person, so I'd enjoy mixing with customers."

"Loves to cook. Mixing with customers," he put down. Then he started writing down the disadvantages: "Long hours. Especially long hours at night. Seven-days-a-week job. Weekend work. High overhead. Labor intensive. Large investment."

"We may as well stop right here," Jay said. "There's no way we can afford to open a restaurant."

"Let's talk about a sewing business," I volunteered. "I could do dressmaking and alterations in the house. This way I'd always be there for the girls. I'd work around their schedule—while they were in school, after they went to bed. Plus there's no overhead."

On the next sheet of paper he wrote in bold letters, "Sewing business."

The advantages side listed: "Loves to sew. No overhead. Flexible hours." In the disadvantages column: "Tedious work. Too confining. Limited opportunities to hire employees. Limited outreach to impact lives." He studied the lists and pronounced, "Minuses far outweigh the pluses."

"Let's scratch sewing," I volunteered.

"Next?"

"How about a catering business?" I suggested. "Again, I could work it around my schedule. Unlike a restaurant, I could do it part time around the girls' school hours and be there for them when they came home in the afternoon. And I wouldn't be stuck with a large overhead because I could do the cooking right here at home."

As I spoke, Jay jotted down everything on the advantages side of a new page. Then we discussed the disadvantages. We concluded that a catering business involved too much evening work, particularly on weekends. "And your busiest times of the year would be on holidays," Jay said. "You'd never tolerate being away from the family on holidays."

"It's too much like the restaurant business," I said. "Scratch that one too."

I even suggested starting a cooking school. "It combines my two loves—cooking and teaching," I told Jay. "What do you think?"

"Sounds interesting. But you'll need a facility with a large kitchen and the overhead could eat up all your profits—no pun intended."

I appreciated Jay's advice, but he kept coming up with faults in every job that interested me. "Aren't you being a bit negative on everything I want to do?" I asked him.

"I'm being objective," he said. "It's far better that you know the disadvantages up front than having to learn them the hard way. Be patient, Doris. You'll find something."

A LIGHTBULB TURNS ON

Convinced I should start my own business, one with flexible hours that would allow me to work around my family's needs, I stopped thinking about the prospect of finding a job. Instead I focused on what I'd like to do, and what particular skills I had that would fill a need in the marketplace. I am a home economist, I repeated to myself, and I enjoy teaching. How can I combine these two interests into some kind of work that will generate enough income to make it worth my time? At the same time, I want to make a difference in other people's lives. To do this, I had to come up with a product or service that fills a void. Figuring that out was not a walk in the park.

I had no money to invest. What kind of business could I start with minimal capital? It had to be a business with little overhead because I couldn't afford to pay rent. Obviously it should be home-based. I wanted to stay home as much as I could with my daughters, and go with them to music lessons and field trips. I wanted to be active in their lives. What could I do working out of my house? By working at home, I could be here during the day when the girls were home, and while they're playing or doing their homework, I could work. And when Jay was home at night, I could put in more time. I could also work a few hours after the girls went to bed.

These were my parameters. Now what career would allow me to channel my passion for cooking and teaching into providing a needed service to consumers? One day, while sitting at the kitchen table with Jay, a lightbulb came on. "I have an idea I want to run by you," I said. "My home economics background has made me proficient with tools in the kitchen."

"No argument here," Jay said.

"While it's second nature to me, this is not true with a lot of women. Have you ever noticed that when friends visit us, the women ask me all kinds of questions while I'm preparing food in the kitchen?"

"Truthfully," Jay said, "I never paid any attention to it."

"Sometimes they seem surprised at how I use my kitchen tools to prepare and serve food. What is routine for me evidently is not to them. What I consider simple and basic tools are things that other people don't seem to have in their kitchens. I'm not talking about the kinds of tools a chef would use, such as a special chopping knife. I'm talking about the very basic tools that anyone could use.

" 'Where did you get that pair of scissors, Doris?' they ask. 'I could certainly use one like it. Do me a favor and pick one up for me the next time you see one.' I find it curious that they don't have enough interest to go do it themselves, but they seem to like it after they try it. Jay, I think there's a real need for providing this service to people."

"It's definitely a convenience," Jay encouraged me.

"I think I could sell kitchen tools to women," I continued. "All the tools that are essential to me in our kitchen. A lot of women don't even know they exist." Something else that crossed my mind was that more and more mothers were entering the workforce. I believed that this was a long-term trend. "With full-time jobs, women have less time to spend in the kitchen. I can sell them tools that will make cooking less time-consuming and more pleasant. The products I would sell would be high quality, reasonably priced, and some of them could be multipurpose."

"It sounds like there could be a need," Jay said.

"It's the same story when we go to our friends' homes," I said. "They don't have pie servers, kitchen scissors, proper cutting boards, or the right knives. People give attention to the color scheme in the living room or the design in the kitchen but never to the appropriate tools. Even my mother is like that. I've had to send her things to upgrade her kitchen."

"I think you're on to something here," Jay said, nodding his head with approval. "But how do you intend to sell these products?"

"I don't know," I shrugged. "I'm still thinking about it. I'll come up with something."

COMING UP WITH THE CONCEPT

After a brief discussion with Jay, I ruled out selling kitchen tools in a retail store. Kitchen products sitting on the shelves wouldn't work because people would have no idea what to do with them. The products had to be demonstrated.

I remember when I was in grade school and the Hula Hoop was first introduced. It was one of the first toys advertised on television, and as soon as I saw children demonstrating a hoop on TV, I wanted one. All the kids did. It looked like fun! Later, I read a case history of the manufacturer, Wham-O, and learned that the company initially tried to sell Hula Hoops to retail stores without first advertising them. Consumers who saw Hula Hoops sitting on the shelves had no idea what they were. Do you roll them? Play horseshoes with them? What are they for? So the hoops just sat there gathering dust. Only after kids saw how they worked on TV did they start moving off the shelves.

Later, Wham-O introduced the Frisbee. In 1961, company sales representatives recruited campus representatives who earned extra money by distributing Frisbees to other students and demonstrating how to use them. Frisbees quickly went airborne on campuses everywhere. When the college students went home for spring break, they took their Frisbees with them. Sure enough, when their kid brothers and sisters saw how much fun

Frisbees were, they wanted one too. Imagine seeing a Frisbee for the first time on a store shelf. How would you know what it was? What do I do with it? Is it a plate? Do I flip it? Slide it on the ground? Use it to feed my dog? Do I float it? Unless you saw one demonstrated, you'd have no interest in buying a Frisbee.

For the same reason, the products I had in mind would not sell in stores, nor could they be only sold in catalogs. Displaying a picture of them would be as ineffective as placing them on shelves in a store. Besides, the cost of starting a catalog company was almost as much as opening a retail store. So I ruled out starting a mail-order business.

I concluded that my products definitely had to be demonstrated. This was evident to me because so many women didn't know how to use kitchen tools, despite their availability in retail stores. In this respect, they were no different from the Hula Hoop or the Frisbee. But unlike Wham-O's products, I couldn't pass them out on college campuses. In a process of elimination, I concluded the best way to sell my products would be through in-home demonstrations, like those provided by companies such as Tupperware and Mary Kay Cosmetics. The ideal place to demonstrate them would be in the privacy of someone's kitchen, where a group of friends could get together in a relaxed atmosphere. Over the years, I had attended various direct-selling companies' parties, so I was familiar with how the party-plan system worked. I had trouble, however, seeing myself conducting a party to sell kitchen tools.

But the more I thought about the idea, the more I could visualize myself in the kitchen in front of a small group of women. It would be similar to a home economics extension course. I would conduct a kitchen class, and attendees would be invited to participate. I'd teach the women how to properly use great kitchen tools. There would also be an exchange of recipes—I would offer recipes and tips on easy-to-prepare, delicious meals, and the attendees could also exchange recipes. Participation is an excellent way to learn. While I had no real sales background, I viewed selling as a form of teaching. And my teaching background would be a plus here.

"I'll go to my customers' homes and teach women what to do. And if they have any questions, I'm right there to answer them," I told Jay. "I want to make the kitchen tools come alive."

"I like the idea," he replied. "You'll have little overhead and you can work out of the house, and keep a limited amount of inventory in the basement that you can restock as needed."

"How much inventory do you think I'll need?"

"Let's first figure out what products you want to sell," Jay replied.

As things turned out, the amount of inventory I initially kept in my basement was determined in part by the limited amount of money we had to put into the business. Jay volunteered to borrow $3,000 from the cash value of a life insurance policy on his life. While I had grown up believing that the money put into a life insurance policy should never be touched, I reluctantly agreed that's where we'd get the money. After all, how else could I start my own business?

THINKING OUTSIDE THE BOX

Although I had attended direct-selling parties, I had never worked for a direct-sales company. I had been a host only once, and it was a bad experience—I was embarrassed by the pressure put on friends to book a party. In reality, I knew very little about direct selling. And what I did know, I must admit, was a bit of a turnoff.

"I was never interested in direct selling, because the salespeople always came across as pushy," I told Jay. "They must have been trained to apply high pressure. I always felt obligated to buy something."

"Why would you feel obligated?"

"Because I was at a friend's house. Do you remember that crystal houseware products party I went to with one of my girlfriends? We sat through the entire party, and there wasn't a single thing either of us wanted. First, I didn't think the crystal was good quality. Second, when a price list was passed around the room, I thought the products were overpriced. The two of us decided to buy the cheapest thing listed, a $14.95 set of candleholders. I whispered to my girlfriend, 'Let's split the order. You take one and I'll take the other one because they can be used individually.' I didn't even want the one candleholder, but it was a graceful way to buy something and get out without embarrassment. I suspected that the company purposely didn't have anything less expensive, so its salespeople could bring in more money from the people who attended. I would never want someone to feel that way on my behalf."

"What else do you object to about direct sales?" Jay asked.

"The company representative continually urged us to buy more so that the hostess would receive more products. Don't you think it's tacky to invite people to a party at your house, and pressure them to buy? I certainly do. I'll tell you something else I don't like. There are too many gimmicks, too much game playing. Their presentations are all about making people feel obligated. Personally, I don't like making people feel uncomfortable. You know me, Jay—that's not me."

"It can't be that bad."

"You've never been to one of these things," I said, a bit irritated. "You haven't seen how they push you to buy. How they make the woman hosting the party feel like crawling under the sofa because they say, over and over, 'If one of you would step up and book a show, your friend will get this and this. But if nobody steps up, she's not going to get it.' "

Jay gave me a bewildered stare. "But why do you have to do all those things? Just do whatever you want to do."

"But that's what direct selling is all about," I said. "If you're in that business, you've got to have weekly meetings of your sales force. You've got to teach them high-pressure tactics."

"No, you don't."

"I'll tell you what," I said, raising my voice. "The next time I get an invitation, I'm sending you. You just don't know how these things work because you've never been to one."

"Hey, don't get mad at me," Jay said. "I'm not denying what you say. All I'm saying to you is, do it your way. And if you object to something, change it!"

"You don't get it, Jay," I said. "That's what direct selling is. I can't change the way it's done."

"Yes, you can."

"Jay, you don't get it."

"No, *you* don't get it, Doris," Jay shot back at me. "If you're going to start your own business, you can do it any way you want. The chalkboard is wiped clean. This is your business. You don't play games. You don't use high pressure. You do this or that— whatever you want to do. You do it because it's *your* business."

Suddenly that lightbulb came on. It was so obvious. Jay was right. I was looking at it, saying, "The box has four sides." He was looking at it and saying, "The box can be any shape you want it to be." I had not allowed myself the freedom to think outside the box. Of course it was my business! I could do it any way I wanted! I didn't have to emulate what other direct-sales companies did. That was a defining moment for me. I realized I could cut loose those constraints that I had believed came with the home party package. From that point on, I knew exactly what I wanted to do.

Consumed with enthusiasm and excitement, I could barely sleep at night. I couldn't stop thinking about getting into the business!

Later, a few friends advised me to work for a direct-sales organization for a few months before I ventured off into my own business. "You're bound to pick up some ideas," one friend suggested. "Let them train you."

I decided it wouldn't be necessary, because I had no intention to work for one of those companies. I knew enough from the few parties I had attended to feel comfortable bypassing an apprenticeship. I was anxious to get started, and while I could have picked up a few tips, I preferred to learn from my own experiences. Besides, I didn't want to pick up bad habits. The products I wanted to offer were very clear to me. I really had to create my own home party the way I wanted to do it, or not do it at all.

Although I didn't like some things that went on at direct-selling parties, I owe a great debt of gratitude to early companies in the industry, because I didn't come up with the idea on my own. I give credit to companies like Stanley Home Products, Tupperware, Mary Kay Cosmetics, and Rubbermaid, to name a few. Clearly they created the model. I just altered it to fit my own personal style.

I DID IT MY WAY

I decided to conduct my cooking demonstrations with an interesting presentation that would both inform and entertain those present. It would be an evening of refreshments and entertainment with friends. Unlike cooking classes that require women to make a commitment by signing up for a series of classes, my customers would come away from a Kitchen Show with tips on what they saw and learned that night, as well as easy-to-prepare, time-saving recipes.

Right from the start, my plan was to sell only quality products. At the shows I would explain why they were excellent values. At the time, many party-plan companies were selling poor-quality products that I felt were overpriced. I wanted to present a great product at a fair and competitive price. I knew that good-quality products didn't have to cost more. I knew that you could spend the same amount on a well-made vegetable peeler as you'll spend on the one you'll grumble over every time you use it.

I planned to have a wide selection of affordable kitchen tools; I would even offer a cake tester priced at 75 cents. I wanted to have a dozen or so items under $10. A lot of people go to these parties to socialize; they don't want to feel obligated to buy something that costs more money than they'd like to spend. I didn't want anyone going home from a Kitchen Show feeling the way I felt at the crystal housewares party. I vowed never to put pressure on anyone to buy. Regardless of whether they made a purchase, they'd come away with some meal preparation and cooking ideas, plus tips and techniques to assure them that attending a Kitchen Show was time well spent. I also wanted them to tell their friends about the wonderful time they had. If they were turned off because they felt pressured, that would be the kiss of death.

I was determined to keep it simple, so I stayed away from haute cuisine. I wanted the recipes to be simple and fast and produce dramatic results. I wanted people to see that they could achieve the same results with the tools I offered.

At heart, my Kitchen Show would be a show-and-tell presentation. I would demonstrate tools with food so that people could try them out to see if they would work for them. It was to be a try-before-you-buy experience.

Most of all, I wanted to make a difference in people's lives. I strongly believe it is important for families to share meals together. The table provides a setting for drawing families close together at mealtime, through conversation and laughter. The table is where we mark milestones, divulge dreams, bury hatchets, make deals, give thanks, plan vacations, and tell jokes. It is where we live between bites. My business was more than selling kitchen tools. My mission was to bring families together. Admittedly, I didn't even know what a mission statement was back in 1980, but I did have a vision in mind. I could serve people in a truly meaningful way. This thought, more than anything else, excited me. In fact, so much I could hardly fall asleep at night and couldn't wait until the morning to get out of bed and make it happen.

SELECTING A NAME

Jay and I were visiting Harriet and Emory Nelson, good friends of Jay's parents, one evening. Emory had retired after a successful career in advertising and printing. The Nelsons had heard I was serious about starting a business. Emory asked, "You guys got a name for your company?"

"Not yet," I replied. "We haven't thought about it yet."

"Let me help you come up with one," he volunteered.

For the next few hours, we brainstormed and tossed around some names.

"What do you think of Doris's Kitchen?" someone suggested.

"Sounds good. How about the Coddled Cook?"

"Not bad," I said.

Somewhere in the conversation, I mentioned that I planned

to pamper my customers, and from there, The Pampered Chef came up.

Throughout the conversation, Emory was doodling on a notepad. "Take a look at these logos," he said.

One was a chicken sitting on a chef's hat with the words "The Pampered Chef" appearing on the front. Another showed an artichoke with a banner over it with our name inscribed. A third logo was a hen and a chef's hat with a hand over it.

"Let's go with the first one," I said. And so we did.

For the next twenty years or so we used that logo on everything we produced. Every label and every catalog had that hat and hen. It wasn't until we celebrated our twentieth anniversary, in 2000, that we created a more contemporary logo and removed the hen. We felt that the chef's hat, sans hen, was more indicative of cooking. After the change, so many people commented that they could never understand why we had a hen sitting on a hat, as if it were squashing it!

ELEVEN TIPS FOR START-UP ENTREPRENEURS

Having survived the trial and error of launching my business, I offer the following eleven tips for anyone considering starting his or her own company.

1. *Follow Your Passion*
I loved working in the kitchen, and I loved teaching. With my business, I was able to combine these two passions. When I was in college I was able to get through difficult math and science courses because I knew I had to in order to graduate as a home economics major. The same is true in business. There are some

chores that you as an entrepreneur must endure. If you are passionate enough about the other facets of the business, you will put up with what you don't particularly enjoy. If you find something you love, I assure you that your work will be considerably easier.

I believe that one of the key elements to success in business, and in life, is having a passion for what you do. My passion for my work plays a vital role during difficult times; it fortifies my resilience and ability to overcome obstacles, supports my dedication to remain true to my original vision, and fuels my determination to succeed.

When I had the privilege of meeting the legendary Warren Buffett, he told me, "I love my work. I love coming to work every day. I love it so much, I skip to work." I know he truly loves what he does, and because of that, to him it's not work. I feel the same way. What I do is not work—it's a pleasure and a privilege. I was not the smartest or most talented of the people I went to school with. A lot of people who knew me are quick to credit my success to luck or being at the right place at the right time. But that's not it at all. I was blessed to find something I love to do. There's no limit to what you can accomplish when you feel passionate about it. If you excel in a particular area and can channel it into a business, chances are you are going to do it better than your competition.

2. Have a Clear Idea about What You Want to Do

As a small business owner, you must understand what your customer wants. This means asking yourself hard questions: Is there the need for your service? What are realistic charges for your service? What are you seeking to do? What are your objectives, both in what you plan to provide to others that is marketable and what you hope to get out of it for yourself? Where are you going to operate? You must also have a realistic view of what your start-up costs will be. And most important, you must focus on your core business. Many distractions will present themselves, tempting you to diversify—beware. If your business shows promise, wear blinders. As Tom Peters repeatedly says in his best-selling book *In Search of Excellence,* "Stick to the knitting." You can chase a million trails or you can focus on one. If you're sure your idea is a good one, don't deviate from it. I recall a bakery in Chicago that had a message on its doughnut package: *Keep your eye upon the donut and not upon the hole.* Good advice for a start-up entrepreneur.

3. Find a Niche

In today's competitive marketplace, it's not possible to be all things to all people. What's more, it takes vast resources to dominate your marketplace. If multibillion-dollar companies can't do it, neither can your start-up company. Even large, established companies look for ways to fill a niche. To the novice entrepreneur, I recommend you find a niche—offer a service that isn't currently being filled. Interestingly, some niches are too small for big corporations to pursue, but these same niches provide excellent opportunities for a small businessperson.

A small entrepreneur can provide personal service because he or she is the owner of the business. An owner of a small restaurant, for example, can personally greet his customers, know them by name, and even recall their favorite foods and beverages. This personal touch builds customer satisfaction and loyalty. In a crowded marketplace, sometimes it appears there are no niches. But if you look hard, you'll find a need that isn't being properly filled. Many well-intentioned friends told me there was no more room in the marketplace to sell kitchen tools. "Doris, what you plan to sell is available in hardware stores, supermarkets, mail-order catalogs, and even drugstores," I was told. "There is no shortage of places to buy your products." I already knew that. I also knew that consumers could be better served by having kitchen tools demonstrated in a friendly environment. The uniqueness of the way I planned to present my products was my niche. I could provide a value add they were not getting elsewhere.

4. Be the Best You Can Be

I have always had a simple goal: to be the best I can be at what I do. So should you. For the vast majority of us, this isn't such a difficult task because most work isn't rocket science. Martin Luther King, Jr., put it eloquently when he said, "If a man is called a street cleaner, he should sweep the streets even as Michelangelo painted or Beethoven composed music or Shakespeare wrote poetry. He should sweep streets so well that all the hosts in heaven and earth will pause to say, 'Here lived a great street sweeper who did his job well.' "

5. Make a Difference

From the reactions of my friends who spent time with me in my own kitchen, I knew from the start that my services were needed. Knowing I could make a meaningful contribution was important to me. It goes much further than teaching women how to use kitchen tools to prepare meals faster and easier. What I could do at a Kitchen Show went beyond the kitchen. The real benefit to the customer is the carryover effect the Kitchen Show has on his or her family. This is what this business is about—bringing family and friends together at the table during mealtime. This is the real contribution I felt I could make to improve people's lives. It reminds me of when I was a teacher. The salary was secondary to the impact I could have on the students. It's not about punching the clock, taking home a paycheck. If that's all there is to teaching, at some point I'd say, "There must be a better way to earn more money." It's the job satisfaction that truly matters.

I also realized other women might join me in the future, and they too could enjoy a rewarding career with flexible hours, enabling them to work around their family's needs. Like me, they could be home for their children after school, be with their children when they were home sick, and so on. At the same time, they could make better-than-average pay per hour for their work. Knowing I could make a significant difference in the lives of future Pampered Chef Kitchen Consultants inspired me to succeed. Although I started my business to put money away for my children's education and to make a difference in Julie's and Kelley's lives, I was never driven by money. In fact, for nearly ten years, I did not pay myself a salary from the company. Everything I earned went back into the business. With this in mind, I advise new entrepreneurs: if you chase the money, you'll never get it; but if you chase after your dream to serve others, the money will follow you. Find something to do with a purpose that goes beyond just earning a living, beyond just supporting yourself. This is what will drive you to do your very best.

6. Keep It Simple

Or, as Jay says, "KISS—Keep It Simple, Sweetie. Stick to the basics. If you do, everything else will fall into place." With everything that goes on around us, it's easy to get sidetracked by distractions. The secret is to do what you do best and stick to it. Don't make things more complicated than they are. It sounds easy, but evidently it's not as easy as it sounds, because people all over tend to complicate what is otherwise uncomplicated.

When I started my business, I figured I'd market the very serious cook—the woman totally into cooking. At the first Kitchen Show, I quickly discovered my typical customers were a cross section of people, not just the individual who fancied herself a creative, gourmet cook. It's not that my company doesn't appeal to the gourmet cook or the individual with excellent, creative cooking skills, but it goes beyond that customer. Had I limited my product line to this particular customer, I would have missed the opportunity to reach a much larger market of women looking for uncomplicated, simple ways to prepare their family meals. Interestingly, I discovered that even people who say they don't like to be in the kitchen are attracted to our company. Since our products can reduce the time a person spends in the kitchen, we've got something for people who hate to cook, too. The moral here is that as a start-up entrepreneur, you should not overcomplicate what you sell. Confused customers have difficulty making buying decisions. Remember: KISS.

7. Watch Your Overhead

With a bankroll of only $3,000, I didn't have any choice—I had to watch my overhead. It taught me discipline, which I have been mindful of throughout my business career. Of course, even with a small bankroll, with credit, the temptation to overspend is always present. Simply put, don't do it! Establish a budget and stick to it. As I will reveal in Chapter 4, I kept my overhead down. For several years I worked out of my house until it was bursting at the seams. It's easy to spend money; anyone can do it. It's more difficult not to spend. Oftentimes, start-up entrepreneurs who get off to a good start find success goes to their heads. They want to let the world know they've done well; they want to impress people, they overspend. In a matter of time, high overhead takes such a heavy toll that the entrepreneur is unable to withstand even a short downturn in business. Don't let this happen to you.

8. Go with Your Instincts

In the beginning, I operated on sheer instinct. Yes, Jay was there for me to bounce ideas off, but in the end, if we didn't agree, I made the final decision. Over the years I have found my intuition and instincts about my business are seldom wrong. If I have to work too hard to sell myself on an idea, it's probably not a good idea. Unless Jay strongly objected and convinced me of a flaw in my judgment, I stuck with my intuition. Jay respected my intuition even when it didn't make good business sense to him. Was my intuition always right? Of course not! No entrepreneur is ever 100 percent right. If you're always right, then you're not taking enough risks. Fortunately, my batting average was high enough that I learned to trust my intuition.

9. Value Your Time and Be a Good Time Manager

When you run a small business, there is always something to do and never enough time to get it all done. To remain sane and balance your career and family, you must place a high value on your time and use it wisely. My family was my number one priority, and working out of my home, I fit my career around my children and husband. As a consequence, I wore many hats, sometimes several at once! There were times when I'd be doing paperwork or working with my inventory stored in the basement, while traveling back and forth to the kitchen preparing dinner for my family. In between tasks, I would help the girls with their homework or do laundry and other household chores. To get everything done meant eliminating virtually all television, book reading, and social life. Studies estimate that the average person watches three to four hours of television a day. It's amazing what you can accomplish by putting those hours to valuable use. Most people waste more time than they spend working. Once you realize what a precious commodity time is, it's amazing how much you can get done.

10. Brush Up on Your Computer Skills

It's a different ballgame today than it was when I started my business in 1980. Back then, nobody had a personal computer and the Internet did not exist. Today both are essential tools in business. I must confess, my computer skills are weak, which I trace back to my poor showing in typing class. I never learned the proper way to type, so I just peck away with my index fingers on the keyboard—as you can imagine, very slowly. Fortunately, I have support people around me with excellent computer skills, so I don't have to depend on them myself. I realize, however, that I must develop better computer skills, which are necessary even away from the business—in my personal life. So for anyone starting a business today, your computer skills are essential. This same advice applies to anyone who is returning to the workplace. We live in a computer-driven business world, and computer skills will play an even bigger role in the future.

11. It's Only a Business

There were times when I was stressed and overwhelmed with work, and Jay would say to me, "It's only a business."

"But Jay—" I'd start to say, and he'd interrupt, "Doris, this is still only a portion of your entire life. Don't get so hung up with it. Don't take yourself so seriously."

What wonderful advice. This is not to say that I always appreciated hearing it. When I got wrapped up in the business, it was hard to take a breather and unwind. Fortunately that's what I eventually learned to do. Thinking that it was only a business put things in perspective. My family was my number one priority. They are the reason why I started the business. Sure, on rare occasions I become so focused on a pressing problem that I momentarily put the business before my family. But it happens rarely, and whenever I catch myself falling into that trap, I say to myself, "Doris, it's only a business!" Then I feel at peace with myself again.

3
STARTING ON THE
GROUND FLOOR

"Our three-bedroom home is hardly big enough for the four of us. I'm not sure there's room to run a business from it," I told Jay.

"How about setting up shop in the basement?" he suggested.

"You've got to be kidding. It's already cramped down there. Besides, it's dark and dreary and it's full of stuff."

"I'm sure I can fix it up a bit," Jay said. "And besides, the basement is the quietest place in the house. You'll also have space to store inventory."

From the beginning, Jay emphasized the importance of controlling the inventory. "It's crucial in business," he reminded me.

I was a teacher with no experience selling products, so thank goodness for Jay's business background. We agreed I'd buy and sell merchandise and he'd be my inside guy, doing the books, managing the inventory, and so on.

Our unfinished four-hundred-square-foot basement had a six-and-a-half-foot ceiling; the ducts, pipes, and insulation were exposed. Opposite the furnace and hot water tank sat my desk, next to some makeshift shelving Jay had assembled. Except when I ran a load through the washer and dryer, it was as quiet as he said it would be. Once a phone was installed in the basement, I felt like a real businessperson. And with the $3,000 we borrowed on the cash value of Jay's life insurance policy, my checking account had its biggest balance ever.

My game plan was to purchase high-quality kitchen tools like the ones I personally used. I'd sell them by showing small groups of women how to use them. Ever since I came up with the Pampered Chef idea, I had been writing down thoughts about potential products in my loose-leaf notebook. My list started with twenty-five items from my own kitchen that I couldn't live without, and it grew from there. Finally, with a full notebook, I was ready to embark on my first buying trip.

First, I made sure to call Harriet Nelson, a good friend of Jay's parents. She owned Daffy Down Dilly, a small gift shop in Glen Ellyn. I hoped Harriet would fill me in on what I needed to know to buy merchandise. I told her briefly about what I wanted to do and asked, "What do you think?"

"Sounds like it should work," she said enthusiastically. "Go for it!"

"Have any tips on where I can buy my inventory?"

"The Chicago Merchandise Mart, of course!" she exclaimed. "It's probably the best place in the world to find what you're looking for. And best of all, it's right here in Chicago."

Like all Chicagoans, I had heard of the famous Merchandise Mart, a well-known city landmark just north of the Loop. "I've never been there. What do I do? I can't just walk in and shop, can I? Isn't it strictly wholesale?"

"That's right," she said. "The vendors sell only to merchants. You can't get in without a pass."

"A pass? What a shame. I would love to visit the Mart."

"Oh, don't worry, Doris, I'll get you a pass. Just leave it to me."

MY FIRST VISIT TO THE MERCHANDISE MART

The Merchandise Mart was built in 1929 by Marshall Field, founder of Chicago's best-known department store. Its completion fulfilled the famed merchant's dream of having a single wholesale center, with the capacity to serve the entire nation, housed under one roof. Twenty-five stories high, with 4.2 million square feet of floor space, the Mart spans two entire city blocks. The world's largest commercial building, it is also the world's largest trade center.

That hot Friday morning in August 1980, I arrived when the Mart first opened, planning to do all my buying by midafternoon and still make it home in time to prepare dinner. When I walked into the Mart, I felt an immediate rush of disorientation. The place was massive. I thought, *Okay, I'm in. What do I do now?* It reminded me of that insecure feeling I had on my first visit to the campus at the University of Illinois. Fortunately, the Mart had directories, brochures, and maps readily available. I picked up a handful and frantically studied them. I looked for vendors who sold kitchen products, starting with names of products I recognized. Unfortunately, I was familiar with only a handful of brand-name manufacturers and didn't know the names of any distributors. This compounded my confusion because most of the showrooms were for distributors and manufacturer's representatives who carried many different product lines. I was looking for needles in a haystack. I had to wander through a myriad of showrooms in search of specific products I had in mind.

The Mart was not as I had imagined it. It was quite stately, with plush carpeting, not filled wall-to-wall with noisy people. On the contrary, it was very hushed. I noticed many interior decorators escorting their clients from showroom to showroom, while other buyers strolled through the building in twos and threes. Many people seemed to know each other and greeted acquaintances in the showrooms. Showroom staff not working with buyers sat at desks, either doing paperwork or placing telephone calls. And for the most part, the showrooms did not have what I was looking for.

Observing other people in the showrooms and listening to conversations, I realized that my $3,000 bankroll was small potatoes compared to the budgets of department store and chain store buyers who frequented the Mart. And the entire $3,000 couldn't be put into inventory. I had other start-up expenses, ranging from stationery to long-distance phone calls. I knew better than to mention my limited financial resources to a single soul in the entire building, for fear I'd be immediately escorted to the main entrance and instructed, "Don't come back!"

I was used to walking into a department store and having a clerk wait on me, but in the Mart I was rarely approached by anyone. A few salespeople said, "Let me know if I can do anything for you," but that was it. For the most part, I just looked around and didn't attract much attention. I eavesdropped on conversations between other buyers and the vendors. "I'll take three gross of this, four dozen of that, and give me six dozen of this, this, and this." I didn't see anyone buying small lots of threes or sixes as I had in mind. Because I was looking for as many as sixty to a hundred different items, simple math drastically limited the quantities I could afford. To top it off, some buyers were placing orders far in excess of $3,000 for a single item!

When I finally had the courage to speak to a showroom salesperson, I timidly asked, "What is the lowest number of units I can buy of this item?"

"One dozen, ma'am."

"And this one?"

"Same thing."

"Can I buy six of each?"

"One dozen is our minimum per item."

One clerk even told me, "There is also a minimum for re-orders."

It soon occurred to me that vendors were in effect saying, "I'm sorry but I don't know if I even want to bother with you. So make it worth my while. If you prove yourself, maybe I'll let you order and eventually reorder."

I was petrified that someone might mistake me for a house-wife on a shopping spree, buying things for her own kitchen at wholesale prices. How could I prove that I wasn't? If someone were to challenge me, I had no credentials, not even a business card. Nor was there a single person in the building who could vouch for me. Whenever someone took notice of me, the thought raced through my mind that he or she might say, "You don't belong here. You better leave now or I'll have to report you."

After a few more stops at other showrooms, I realized that my imagination was getting the best of me. I was overreacting. I began to notice a few people buying in low quantities similar to what I had in mind. I had been briefed by Harriet, so I was not surprised to hear that there were restrictions on the size of an opening order. Some vendors refused orders under $200, but others required just $100 or only $50 to open a new account. And there were a few that didn't have a minimum. Since I hadn't established a line of credit with anyone, I had to pay by cash or check for everything I purchased. Thankfully, nobody refused to accept a check from me—and to my surprise, nobody asked for my driver's license for identification.

While there were hundreds of showrooms, only a few had what I was looking for, and those few were scattered far and wide. I might find one on the fifteenth floor, and another on the sixteenth floor. Determined to buy some merchandise, I kept walking around, still bewildered but slowly adjusting to the lay of the land. Still, it was taking longer than I had anticipated to make headway. It was frustrating because my expectations had been so high. I had been told, "The Mart has everything. If you can't find it at the Mart, you probably won't find it anywhere. Period." But the place was so enormous that a person could walk miles and miles there in a day's time. No wonder I was getting tired.

Eventually I found a few items I wanted that were affordable because they were available in small quantities. For example, I purchased some cutting boards, towels, and a flour sifter. I also discovered that if I couldn't find a particular brand of something on my list, I was able to buy a comparable item of the same quality made by another manufacturer. Even back then, I knew enough about the materials and construction to determine a product's quality.

A GOOD START AT THE MART

By midafternoon, I found myself wandering into showrooms I had passed on the first round. In just a few hours, I had looked at more merchandise than I had seen in my entire lifetime! My head was spinning, and I was beginning to lose my focus. Then I discovered the Trade Associates Group's showroom. Its attractive display, consisting mainly of colorful towels and aprons, was an attention grabber. In addition to its own products, TAG represented other manufacturers.

In the back of the showroom, I found a display of pizza products—and I really like pizza. There were about ten items including a metal Chicago-style pizza pan, a pizza cutter, and some spatulas. But two items that really caught my eye were a flat pizza baking stone and a deep-dish stoneware pizza vessel. Each was cleverly packaged in a takeout-style pizza box. Great marketing, I thought. One was thirteen inches in diameter and the other was eleven inches by one and a half inches deep. I picked up the first one and read its use and care information. It was in a handwritten style and designed to be artful rather than informative. It also had some recipes, and again I surmised they were just for show. For instance, it left out the time the pizza should be baked in the oven. The more I read, the more confusing it was.

I must have spent enough time studying these pizza stones that I looked like a serious buyer. An unenthusiastic saleswoman finally noticed me and said, "So do you like those things?"

"Oh, gosh," I answered. "I've seen pizza things before and these are wonderfully packaged. If I may, I have some questions."

The woman probably thought I wanted to talk price and quantity, because she suddenly perked up.

"Have you ever made anything on these?" I asked.

She politely said, "Pardon me?"

"Have you used these stones personally?"

"Never."

"Do you have to grease them?"

"I'm sorry but I can't answer that question."

"At what temperature do you put them in the oven?"

From her body language, I sensed I was asking the wrong questions. She clearly withdrew from me. To each of my questions, she'd answer, "I have no idea." "I've never used them." "No, no, no."

"Oh, that's too bad," I said. "I would love to talk to somebody who has used them."

"I'm sorry, but I can't help you," she said, and excused herself.

I pored over the brochures, searching for solid information. I picked up each stone to see how much it weighed, trying to get a feel for it. Every now and then, I glanced around for someone who would be able to answer my questions. Eventually, the saleswoman approached me a second time. And again, after a round of questions, I heard, "I don't know. I just don't know." This time when she walked away, she threw her hands into the air.

Apparently my line of questions was unlike anything anyone had ever asked her. I was asking questions that a consumer would ask, not a professional buyer. She wasn't expected to know what I wanted to know!

After two hours in this showroom, I saw a distinguished-looking gentleman walk out of the back office and approach me. Although he was casually dressed, I had the impression he was the saleswoman's supervisor. "So you're interested in the stones."

"I don't know if I am or not," I answered. "I'm sorry but I don't understand them. I have so many questions. Maybe you can answer my questions."

It was now late in the afternoon on a Friday, and he had no doubt been briefed by the saleswoman. Before I could say anything more, he said, "I don't know anything about these."

"I just want to talk to somebody who does," I said, trying to be patient and polite. "Who does? I've never seen anything like them. They're so intriguing."

"Why don't you just take them home with you, ma'am," he said condescendingly. "Try them out and you can get back to us."

Meanwhile, I was thinking that they were priced at $6 apiece, with a minimum purchase of a dozen. So not only was I worried about how they worked, I was concerned about putting out $72 for them. I certainly could not afford to buy anything that I might not even want in my line. But taking them home to do a test run? That was a horse of a different color. I had nothing to lose. If they didn't work, I could return them. Still, I didn't want to impose on his generosity.

"No, I couldn't do that."

"Please, ma'am, take them home with you. Try them out and you can get back to us."

After the stressful day I'd had, I was touched by his magnanimous offer. During the time I had been at the Mart, no one else had seemed so considerate. Oh, I get it now, I thought. He wants me to test them and report back on what I learn so he can pass this information on to other customers. That seemed reasonable. Now here's a smart businessman!

I promised him I'd be a good steward of those stones. And yes, I'd return the favor by bringing back the stones—along with my valuable findings.

"Don't worry about it," he said.

I wanted him to know I had no intention of stealing the stones. "I will see you on Monday."

"It's really not necessary for you to come back so soon. It's perfectly okay to call me whenever you get around to it," he insisted. "Now, it's Friday afternoon, and I want to start closing up a little early, so here are your stones and enjoy your weekend."

I put the two stones in my tote bag. As he ushered me out, I thanked him profusely. A little while later, I realized I had left behind the instructions for one of the stones, but when I went back, the showroom had already been closed up tight.

Later I realized that he had let me take the stones so he could get rid of me and close for the weekend. He would have been perfectly happy if I hadn't returned them at all.

I took public transportation—the Elevated—home, feeling like the mouse that stole the cheese. I was so excited. I read what directions I had several times, trying to figure out what wasn't there. The directions suggested making quiche, pizza, and even cookies. That evening, I tried pizza, frozen pizza, and cookies; I even baked some bread. I got up early on Saturday to test the stones some more, and by noon I was completely sold on them. They were wonderful. My family ate a heavy diet that weekend.

Eager to check in, I called TAG on Monday at 8:00 a.m. No one answered. I tried every half hour, and a little after ten, someone answered the phone. "Hi, this is Doris Christopher," I said. "I'm the woman who borrowed the kitchen stones on Friday afternoon. I have wonderful results to report."

The man interrupted me and said he had no idea what I was talking about.

"Did you notice two stones missing in the pizza display area?"

"No ma'am, I didn't notice."

I placed an order for a dozen of each stone at $6 apiece.

I made several more trips back to the Mart during the next few weeks, until September, when I had no more reason to return. Had I lived farther away, it would have been too expensive to travel to Chicago that many times. What would I have done had I started this company from far away? My limited bankroll couldn't have afforded me meals and lodging, much less airfare. So this is one of those blessings I received, a piece of my life's puzzle that fell into place.

IT'S A LONG RIDE TO THE FIRST SHOW

My inventory was in and, thanks to Jay, neatly organized in our basement. For weeks I had been experimenting with different kitchen tools while preparing our meals so that I'd have firsthand experience with my line of products.

Several months earlier, I had confided my plan to sell kitchen tools to Ruth and Ken Niehaus, our longtime church friends. When Ruth asked how I planned to do it, I explained it would be like a Tupperware party, "but with a lot of different twists."

"I've seen you in the kitchen," Ruth said, "so I know you'll be good at it. I'd like to be there for your first demonstration."

"That's great, Ruth! You're such a good friend," I answered. "Say, would you consider having some people come to your house for my first show?"

"Absolutely," she replied. "Just let me know when you're ready to do it."

I thanked her and we set a date for mid-September. But a couple of weeks before the show I had to call Ruth to say I wasn't quite ready. "How's October 15 instead?" I asked. I assured her I'd be ready by then.

With a deadline to meet, I began work on a presentation to sell my wares. I printed it on three-by-five note cards and practiced on Jay and the girls. When I didn't have a live audience, I spoke to myself in front of a mirror and even to crates I set up in the living room. Despite my rehearsals, I confessed to Jay that I was still scared to death.

"Pretend you are teaching school or in front of a meeting. You never had a fear of speaking in a classroom setting. This is the same thing. You'll be terrific," he assured me.

"What if they ask questions . . ."

"What could anyone possibly ask you that you don't know? Don't worry about it. It's a piece of cake."

A few days later I told Jay, "You know, it's time to call Ruth and confirm the show, but I need more time."

"There's plenty of time for you to be ready," he said.

"But the price list needs work."

"I'll take care of it," Jay said. My husband countered my every excuse. There was no way he would let me back down.

A few days before October 15, I tried once more to tell Jay I'd have to call Ruth to cancel. I still remember his firm voice. "Doris, you have a commitment. Besides, we've got three thousand dollars of inventory in our basement. It can't just sit there. You have to sell it."

We sat down at our dinner table on October 15, 1980, as we always did. But this time it was different, because after we finished, Jay said he'd do the dishes while I went off to work. He helped load my Plymouth Volare, cramming six crates of products into it. It was cold and rainy, the kind of night I would have loved to stay home, curled up in bed with a good book.

"You'll do just fine," he reassured me. "Drive carefully."

Ruth Niehaus lived about ten miles from us in Elmhurst, and I had planned to use the driving time to go over in my mind one last time what I intended to say. Suddenly, it struck me—it was show time!

"What am I doing?" I thought to myself. "What have I got myself into? What made me think this would work? I must have been out of my mind."

It was raining cats and dogs, and traffic moved at a snail's pace. "What a miserable night," I said out loud. "How fitting. I must have been deluding myself over the past few months. Boy, I've had some foolish ideas in the past, but this tops them all. This is the worst idea I ever concocted. How can I get myself out of this?"

As I drove nearer to Ruth's house, I thought, *I could pull over and call her to cancel the show. No, that wouldn't be right. Ruth has invited her friends and neighbors. She's expecting me. I have to do this.*

Even as I pulled into her driveway, I thought, *I may do this once, but I'll never, ever do it again. Somehow I'll manage to get through this thing.* I kept visualizing myself as finished. The thought never occurred to me that I had enough inventory to fill forty more crates in my basement. I wasn't even worried about the $3,000 I had put into it. All I wanted was to get through the next couple of hours and be done with it forever.

When I rang the doorbell, Ruth gave me a big welcome. "Scott will help you carry everything in," she offered.

"No, it's my job," I said, "and I'll do it." Why should I make things any worse by having her teenage son mad at me?

"We're going to do this in the basement family room," she said.

The basement stairs were so narrow that I had to maneuver sideways to carry down each of those heavy crates. Six trips back and forth to my car later, I was drenched. Some of the women were already downstairs, and with my back toward them I set up for the show. I didn't want to see anyone's face. *I'll just do it this one time and get it over with,* I promised myself. When everything was set up, I turned around to see a roomful of women, eagerly waiting to hear my story.

THE FIRST KITCHEN SHOW

I was standing in front of a group of nine women in Ruth's family room. The products from my six crates were displayed around me. *Well, here I go,* I thought.

"Hi, my name is Doris Christopher, and I'm starting a new business. It's called The Pampered Chef. I am so pleased you all came. I want to thank Ruth for opening her home. Now I'm going to show and tell you about a lot of things I have with me tonight." And there I was. The first and probably last kitchen show was in progress. *This isn't so bad,* I thought. *I'll be through with it in no time and never have to do this again.*

"Tonight, I'm going to show you how to use these wonderful baking stones," I said. "I came across them this summer, and I adore them. They're like nothing I've ever seen before. Now I'm making the most delicious pizzas you can imagine right in my own kitchen—on a par with or even better than what you can buy in the best pizza parlors in Chicago. I can see from your reactions that you've never seen anything like these stones. Neither had I. But I'll tell you a secret—they've been around a long time. The ancient Egyptians baked in stone ovens and they also baked on rocks placed under the hot sun. These baking stones work on the same principle.

"I asked Ruth to buy a frozen pizza," I continued, "and I've placed it on this stone. Notice the chopped veggies on the top." Their eyes were wide open. In 1980 this was a revolutionary concept.

"Okay, Ruth is going to put this in the oven upstairs, and while it's baking, we'll talk about some other things I have with me. And when the pizza is ready, I'm going to serve it to you. You can judge for yourself how it tastes. Meanwhile, I'm going to cut up some veggies and show you how to make some fancy little garnishes."

The vegetables were placed on a tray with a dip bowl and passed around the room. As I got into it, the next ninety minutes breezed by. The women were having a great time and so was I! It was as if I were teaching one of my old home economics classes. Even better, they listened with rapt attention. It wasn't as if I were in front of a group of students and had to say, "Sit up, you there in the back row!" They were listening. Truly listening. What's more, they were participating. They were passing things around. My goodness, they're even helping me, I thought. When the pizza was ready, I used some of the tools I brought to cut it up. Next, pizza slices were passed to everyone, and they loved them.

"I've never had a frozen pizza taste so good," one woman said excitedly.

"I could do this!" exclaimed another.

"I can't wait to make pizza for my family."

"By the way, you can even bake cookies and bread on these baking stones," I informed them.

Then the questions started. Lots of questions! They were really into it. They were passing the kitchen tools around the room, and handling them and studying them carefully. By the end of the evening, they bought $178 worth of kitchen tools. I was thrilled. More important, four women approached me and asked when they could invite their friends for a kitchen show at their homes.

Driving my Volare home, I thought of what an unbelievable experience I just had. No longer was I wondering how I had got myself into a terrible mess. Instead, I was on cloud nine, thinking about the four kitchen shows that had just been set up—two with women I had previously known and two with women who, only a little while before, had been complete strangers. There was no time now for negative thoughts. I had a show booked for the very next day! And although I had vowed to myself earlier that night that I would never do another, I was looking forward to a repeat performance.

When I pulled into my driveway, I sat there a moment to unwind. Adrenaline rushed through me. Going to Ruth's house took forever, but how did I get home so fast? Actually, with so many thoughts rushing through my head I didn't even remember the drive home. I couldn't wait to tell Jay what happened.

The moment I walked inside the house, Jay greeted me. "How did it go? Tell me everything."

ANALYZING THE FIRST KITCHEN SHOW

There is an old story about a pet food manufacturer about to launch a new line of dog food. His company hires the top specialists in nutrition, packaging, marketing, advertising, and public relations. The company's CEO anticipates a huge success. Large quantities of the dog food are shipped to retailers across the country. For the first three months, sales boom. Three months later, sales have fallen so badly that the dog food division shuts down.

"What went wrong?" the CEO asks his management team. "We did everything right. Our research indicated we'd make millions on our new line of dog food."

"The problem was," says a vice president, "the dogs didn't like it."

Any possible future success depended on my doing successful kitchen shows. Until I actually did one, however, my business plan was strictly theoretical. My first Kitchen Show was the moment of truth. Had it bombed, my business career could have come to a screeching halt. Had the reception to my kitchen tools been weak, I would have been stuck with a basement full of inventory. As Jay said, the downside to my new venture was losing our $3,000 initial investment. Everything was on the line at that first kitchen show.

I didn't set the world on fire with $178 in sales. By today's standards, it was a rather meager show. But it did prove that our concept worked. One thing I hadn't anticipated was how much attendee participation there would be. I had rehearsed my presentation by following a detailed script, but at the actual show people started making comments and asking questions. Rather than a monologue, as I had delivered when I taught in a classroom environment, there was much more back-and-forth between my audience and me. For instance, when I passed a vegetable peeler around, one woman said, "Wow, the one I use is an antique compared to this one. This one is so much better."

Another woman examined it and remarked, "So this is your secret for peeling veggies. I think I need one in my kitchen."

Once everyone got involved, they began to sell to each other. In fact, at times I just sat back and let them do the talking. I listened and learned. When I passed recipes around the room, I let them talk about their own recipes. While I was pleased with the sales I made that first night, I was positively ecstatic about having booked four more shows. Selling merchandise without generating bookings would have been disappointing. But when four women volunteered to host shows, two of them strangers, I knew that I wouldn't have to rely on selling only to my friends and relatives. Had that been the case, it would only have been a matter of time before I ran out of friends and relatives and was out of business. With volunteers coming forward to host their own shows, I envisioned a chain reaction: if other shows mimicked this first one, I'd enjoy ongoing bookings. I learned so much from my first Kitchen Show, and from every one I've done since. Of course, some shows are better than others, but every show is worth doing. This is true even when sales are low. That's because I'm always booking future shows and, now that I'm no longer a one-woman show, getting leads on potential Kitchen Consultants. Above all, I'm always learning something.

MY MENTOR AND TORMENTOR

For the record, I do not refer to my loving husband as "my mentor and tormentor." But he does. Also for the record, I don't know how I could ever have started this business without Jay. It's wonderful having somebody who challenges your thinking the way he did—something he continues to do to this day. I know I ended up at a better place for having thought through the process and assessed his sometimes contrary point of view. I had to decide whether one of us was right, or neither of us was right, or whether a middle position is where we needed to be. Jay caused me to really think about all dimensions of the box because he sees possibilities that I don't see. An extremely creative thinker, Jay is also an excellent facilitator; these skills are not my strong suit. Consequently, he sees opportunities because he's a self-starter. On the other hand, I am a good detail person.

While Jay and I share similar values, we are very different people. For instance, I like routines; I like to have things organized. I am a planner who likes to stick to the script. I'm considered quite predictable and reliable, traits that are real strengths in business. The upshot is that I squeeze a lot into every hour of every day. Jay is more unpredictable and much more spontaneous. At times he may move a little slower than I do, and he doesn't always get as much done—but this serves as one of his assets, because he's able to roll with the punches.

Also, Jay is more of a risk taker than I am. I like to know what I will be doing before I do it. Jay is quick to launch out and try something new; he has no fear of sailing into uncharted waters. Once he buys into a project and loves it, he immerses himself and screens out everything else. Like me, he's a hard worker, but when he's into something, he loses track of the time until he gets it done. I, however, have more peripheral vision; I see all the things going on around me and then I attempt to make everything fit together. I am more organized, and prefer to do work that I must finish within a period of time. I'm good at fitting the puzzle together, always trying to maximize my output. The fact that Jay and I bring different strengths to the table makes us such a good team.

Jay is a masterful devil's advocate. He's always confronting me to look for less-than-obvious solutions. Whenever I approach him with a problem, he tosses out five different ways to tackle it. Then he suggests alternate routes. He frequently says, "You know, Doris, you don't have to hit everything head-on. You don't have to go over it, you can go around it or under it."

Perhaps even more than playing the role of the devil's advocate, Jay has counseled me much as a therapist would. Like a therapist, he asks poignant questions that make me think—and come up with my own answers. He forces me to figure out what possibilities exist and which ones to consider, sometimes just by asking a critical question. At times it is vexing. But during that crucial time, Jay really helped me think through what I did and didn't want to do.

Having no business experience, I must confess that in the beginning, like all start-up entrepreneurs, I had my doubts. I had no idea what to expect, and there were no guarantees that I would succeed, or, for that matter, that I would recoup our $3,000 investment. Jay's enthusiasm and excitement got me through those times when I felt uneasy, unsure that my business concept would work. As I heard Jay say many times in the past, "Nobody ever loses money on paper. The worst-case scenario, Doris, is we lose three thousand dollars. That's the downside, but the upside is enormous in comparison."

From the start, I focused on the sales side of the business and Jay focused on the operational side. In this capacity he constantly repeated, "This is your business for eight to ten hours a day. It is also our home. We need to keep it as neat and clean as possible."

He repeated this so many times, he sounded like a broken record; but he made his point. Interestingly, our business has followed this advice since its commencement. Our floors are always spotless, our inventory is neatly organized and stacked. We never allow it to get sloppy.

BEING A ONE-WOMAN SHOW

I got what I asked for. I was in business for myself and had all of the comforts—and discomforts—of being self-employed. There was no one to tell me what to do. I could work whenever I felt like it. If I didn't feel like working on a particular day, I didn't have to. Plus, I could work my own hours, which gave me the freedom to come and go as I pleased.

It also meant I had to do everything from carrying out the trash to answering correspondence. And remember, back then there was no such thing as e-mail. Not only did I do the selling, I did the buying. This meant trips back and forth to the Mart as well as a lot of other places, to get what I needed from manufacturers, wholesalers, and distributors. And when I couldn't find a product, I just had to do without it—not like today when we design what isn't out there and have it made exclusively for the Pampered Chef line.

The women who attend a Kitchen Show only see the tip of the iceberg. They see other women having fun as they learn to be more efficient in the kitchen. The women are relaxed after a day at work or after being busy all day with their children. There is always something scrumptious to eat. As I said, it is a fun night. At the same time, I too was having a good time at those first shows. I enjoyed the teaching aspect of my work and I thrived on the warm reception I received. Everyone was always so appreciative. It was as if I was on a mission; at every show, I was able to make a difference in the lives of other families. So I felt good about myself. I was doing something worthwhile. This was what women saw, and I'm sure it's what motivated them to ask me if I could do a kitchen show in their homes.

Though a two-to-three-hour Kitchen Show, as I came to call it, was only one part of my day, it was my favorite part—I truly enjoyed doing a show. I always felt high afterward. And since I liked to experiment with new ideas, every show was different, which is why I never got tired of giving them. I enjoyed getting up in front of a receptive audience. It reminded me of being in high school, when I had the lead in the class play. I'm no different from anyone else. Don't we all respond well to applause? It's not that the women applauded me for my performance at a Kitchen Show. Well, actually sometimes they did after I took a scrumptious coffee cake or a mouthwatering pie out of the oven. But the real applause I received was in the orders they placed at the end of the show. I took that as proof of their approval.

By the way, the six crates that I took to each show contained only the products I used for demonstrations. The merchandise in them wasn't something anyone could buy and take home that same day. On Saturdays, Jay and I loaded our cars and made deliveries. We couldn't afford a babysitter, so we'd each take one of our girls. We saw it as a chance to spend some one-on-one time with them. In the car, they would draw, do puzzles, and, as they got older, do homework. Sometimes we'd stop to get ice cream, pick up a book at the library, or buy a toy. Making the deliveries was time-consuming, and when we eventually were able to afford it, we turned delivery over to UPS.

One of our distributors had a large warehouse located in a blighted area near downtown Chicago. I didn't feel particularly safe going there. On days when I had to pick up merchandise

while Jay was at work, I'd drive the family station wagon and
park in the rear of the warehouse, at the loading dock. The guys
loaded boxes in my car so high that I couldn't use my rearview
mirror. The weight of the boxes made the car sag so low that I
had to stay clear of potholes. With so much cargo, the car had
no pickup, and going home, I'd creep slowly along the freeway.
God, please don't let me get a flat tire, I'd pray.

"Are you sure the car can carry this much weight?" I questioned Jay.

"No problem," he'd assure me.

I looked forward to the day when I'd never again have to
haul those heavy loads.

THE SOFT SELL

I have never liked it when a salesperson applied pressure to sell
me, so when I started The Pampered Chef, I was already a strong
advocate of the soft sell. The soft sell is especially important
when the sale takes place in the home of someone who hosts a
kitchen show. I have always been careful to remember I am a
guest in her house. I wouldn't want someone to come to my
house and pressure my friends to buy something, and neither
would anybody else.

My only previous selling experience had been when I worked
part time at Marshall Field's Department Store, selling linens,
women's fashions, and shoes. I didn't consider it selling. I thought
of it as "waiting on people." "May I help you, miss?" "Let me
know if you see something you like." I didn't receive any sales
training, and I had no idea how to apply sales pressure, nor
would I have wanted to. When I started The Pampered Chef, I

sold purely on instinct, which was based on how I would want somebody to sell me.

From a Kitchen Show host's point of view, the shows were a way to enjoy a few relaxing hours with friends. Besides being a fun night with the girls, it was informative. A Kitchen Consultant would demonstrate how to be more efficient in the kitchen. She would give a show-and-tell presentation. If someone saw something useful that she needed in her kitchen, she could buy it. Every product was high quality and often difficult to find in a retail store. If you needed it, this was a convenient way to get it.

I believed the products I had were the best of their kind for the money, and that someone who knew how to use them properly would certainly get his or her money's worth. I loved to cook so I thoroughly enjoyed demonstrating them. Jay believed that it was my enthusiasm that sold them, rather than my selling technique. I agree, because enthusiasm is contagious. I was excited about what I demonstrated and, consequently, the people around me became excited about the products. It was as simple as that.

What's more, putting on a Kitchen Show isn't rocket science. I was doing something anyone could emulate. It wasn't haute cuisine. I liked to keep things simple so people could expect to enjoy the same results in their own kitchens.

A VISIT TO MY HOME OFFICE

During one of my first trips to the Mart, I purchased one of my favorite products, a glass bowl with a spout and a handle that measures two quarts. Because they were big, heavy, and breakable, I wanted to buy them from a distributor in the Chicago area. Anchor Hocking made them, so I wrote to the local distributor, enclosing my business card. Thinking he had a good lead, a salesman called to set up an appointment to visit me.

Since my letterhead and card had a post office box number but no street address, he asked, "Where are you located?"

I gave him my address and directions. "I'll be there Thursday morning at ten-thirty," he said.

At ten-thirty he hadn't shown up. Fifteen minutes later he called to say: "I've been driving up and down Thatcher Avenue, but I can't find your store."

When he told me where he was, I said, "We're right down from the corner."

"I'm confused, ma'am. I have gone by that corner and it's a residential area."

"Oh, I didn't even think to tell you that. I work out of my home."

"Oh," he said. I could hear the disappointment in his voice. "I'm close by; I'll be right there."

When I greeted him at the door, he scratched his head. We sat at my kitchen table and he showed me several products we had discussed during our initial telephone conversation. Looking back, by his demeanor I could tell he was alternately annoyed and amused. At the time I was all business and was so intent on buying that I was simply engrossed in his batter bowls. I bought the minimum that his company would sell to me, and the total order came to $250. I emphasized to him that this was just the beginning of many orders. "Everyone loves your batter bowls, so you can expect a lot of reorders from me, sir."

Was it worth his while to spend his entire morning with me for a $250 order? Probably not. But over time we purchased a large quantity of those batter bowls. When I ran into him at a housewares show years later, I gave him a big hello and said, "I haven't seen you for a long time."

By this time, we had become well known in the housewares industry and had moved to a different location. We chatted for a while and he said, "I'm just amazed at how well you've done, Doris. You know, I'll never forget that day I met with you in your kitchen. I had been thinking it was some sort of a joke, but you were so serious. When I walked out of your house, I was thinking, what a waste of time."

"Well, you were very gracious because you didn't give that impression at all," I told him.

"I'm so glad I didn't," he replied. "But very honestly, Doris, I walked out of your house doubting you could make it. I didn't think you had a snowball's chance in hell. Now, I've told this story dozens of times, and when I talk to young sales reps, I tell them what a good lesson it teaches. I tell them never to prejudge a prospective customer. And to be respectful to the small ones because from little acorns mighty oak trees grow." (To date we have sold millions of batter bowls.)

HAVING A SUPPORTIVE SPOUSE

I have a hard time imagining how a married person can succeed without the support of his or her spouse. I know women who sell real estate and whose husbands give them a hard time every weekend afternoon or evening that they go out to show a property. "What am I and the kids supposed to do for dinner?" one husband demands. "Don't expect me to babysit," says another. "I'll be on the golf course Sunday." What a handicap to work under.

Then when she comes home late, he complains, "Don't tell me you worked all day on a Sunday and didn't make a sale," he says. "What a total waste of time." The last thing a person needs to face after a bad day in the sales field or at the office is even more resistance at home. Your home is supposed to be a sanctuary—a place filled with tranquillity and love.

It's a two-way street. I've seen wives react the same way toward their husbands. A home builder's wife might say, "You lost your shirt on the last house you built on speculation. At the rate you're going, we'll end up in the poorhouse." Each of us needs encouragement, and businesspeople who take risks need positive reinforcement from the home front. What they don't need is someone filling their minds with negative thoughts and self-doubt. To be an entrepreneur, a businessperson must take risks. He or she won't succeed every time at bat. A spouse should build up his or her partner's confidence, not tear it down. Each of us needs to come home to a caring environment that oozes comfort, not distress.

The truth is, I don't know how I would ever have gotten this business past square one without Jay's support. Many evenings when I came home late, even though Jay had to get up early the next morning, he waited up for me. It was always a joy to know that the dishes were cleaned and put away so I didn't come home to a dirty kitchen. Then he'd carry those heavy crates into the house. Afterward, he'd ask how the show went. Jay shared my enthusiasm and loved getting my feedback. Not only did he listen intently, he asked a lot of questions and offered suggestions on alternative ways to conduct future Kitchen Shows.

"How did everyone like the baking stones?" he'd ask. "What did they like the most? Did you book any shows?"

Later on, when we started to build a sales organization, he'd ask, "Did anybody want to become a Kitchen Consultant?"

I never wanted to disappoint Jay, because he always rooted for me to succeed. His actions spoke louder than his words. Besides delivering packages to customers on Saturday afternoons, he'd now and then drive me to a Kitchen Show, carry the crates into the house, and pick me up when it was over. Sometimes, he'd go to a nearby shopping center or take in a movie and stop by afterward to drive me home. Jay would also sometimes drive me to out-of-town trade shows.

Before he left the house in the morning, Jay offered his reminders. "Now don't forget, Doris, you're supposed to call so-and-so to order these products. And be sure to get hold of UPS to schedule the pickups."

Sometimes he'd rattle off a list of a half-dozen things to do. "You don't have to tell me that," I'd say.

"I'm just telling you because we need to continue and build," he'd say. "And you sometimes tend to procrastinate." Yes, he pushed a little hard at times. No question, he could be aggressive. In the end, I knew he always had my best interests in mind and was behind me 100 percent.

Other than an occasional out-of-town trip to a convention, he made sure to be home in time for dinner or by six on the evenings when I would be doing a show. He worked his schedule around mine so he could be with the girls. And most importantly, I could always rely on him. If he said he'd be home at a certain time, I could count on it.

Jay managed the inventory we kept in our basement, and in those days when I was the only Kitchen Consultant, he would remind me how much we had stocked. If we ran low on a certain product, he'd say, "Better show something else today, Doris." Later when we had other Consultants, they assumed that everything was always available, so we had to keep an adequate supply of every item. At that point, we had to grow our inventory, although its turnover decreased.

Jay was a master at organizing our downstairs inventory. When I was doing a show, after he put the girls to sleep, he'd go to the basement and reorganize everything, always making sure to stay on top of our inventory. Sometimes, I'd get irritated at him and say, "Will you stop moving things already?"

"You can never be too organized," he'd reply. Of course, I knew he was right, particularly when he quoted magazine articles citing troubles incurred by big companies that were unable to keep their inventories in order.

After dinner on Sunday nights, the two of us had a tradition, which was to go down to the basement with our price list, and walk down the aisle. That handwritten price list itemized each kitchen tool: cake tester (112 in stock), ten-inch whisk (60 in stock), French scraper (72 in stock), spatter shield (48), gravy strainer (12), and so on. We'd start at the top of the list and count the inventory. He would count how much of each product we had in stock and shout the number for me to write down. Our tabulation of all the orders stored in the house helped us determine the demand for everything. Early on Monday mornings, I placed orders according to what we thought would sell. We did this religiously for all the years the business was home-based. It helped us keep our expenses down and, however primitive, our homemade system was a workable just-in-time inventory. This was all new to me, but to Jay it was second nature.

Did Jay make sacrifices for my work? Absolutely. We both made them. For instance, prior to the business, we played in a pinochle club with six to eight other couples. Once we started the company, our friends noticed that neither one of us paid attention to our cards. Both of us had difficulty focusing on what we were doing because the business was so much on our minds. Eventually we started going to fewer and fewer club meetings. Finally we stopped playing pinochle altogether. We definitely lost contact with some of our friends. Because there simply wasn't enough time to do everything, our social life dropped a level or two. And for years, Jay had been an avid stamp collector, but once the business got started, instead of buying stamps, he put his money into additional inventory. "It was a business decision," he says. "We could generate a profit much faster in this business than with a stamp collection."

A FAMILY AFFAIR

Putting the family first is a central part of our company's philosophy, and it would be hypocritical for me to put the Christopher family in second place behind my work. Family first, career second. This is the order. Always. This doesn't mean there can't be harmony between the two. On the contrary, operating a business in the home becomes a family affair.

Remember, I went into this business so that I could work around my two grade-school daughters' schedules. And I did. I was in car pools to and from school activities, and I was always available in the afternoons when they came home. And if there was a sick child in bed, I was home with her. Like a full-time, stay-at-home mom, I was fully involved with their activities. I was a room mother, the Girl Scout cookie mom—the whole nine yards. When the girls were little, I went to their soccer, basketball, and volleyball games. I was on the sidelines cheering them on. Julie played piano and violin; Kelley played piano and an assortment of other musical instruments. I took them to their practices and made it to all their recitals. And yes, many last-minute business events came up, each of which could have served as a good excuse to opt out of family activities. But I never did. I wanted my girls to know that when one of us said we'd be there, we'd be there. They never had to give it a second thought.

When the girls were old enough, we put them on our payroll. They started out stamping the Pampered Chef logo on paper bags, and as they got older, they took on more responsibilities. We always paid them and they were never asked to do anything they didn't want to do. In other words, we didn't force the business on them. Admittedly, Jay and I talked about the business at the dinner table, but we made a conscientious effort to avoid too much shoptalk around the girls. Meals together were times to talk about other subjects, including what was going on in Julie's and Kelley's lives. We let them know that their activities were every bit as important as ours. A little business conversation is healthy for children to hear, but there's a fine line, which we tried not to cross.

Of course in spite of our good intentions, Jay and I sometimes overdid it with business talk. He was so excited about my career that he'd sometimes start asking me questions at the dinner table that required more than a brief answer. The girls weren't shy about letting us know how they felt. Kelley once said, "Do we have to talk Pampered Chef tonight? Can't we talk about something else?" Jay and I would glance at each other and quickly change the subject.

Having a front-row seat at the building of a home-based business, the girls received a good education, partly by osmosis, as they saw a little business start humbly and grow and grow and grow. They couldn't help but learn a thing or two about starting a business from scratch. They also learned the joy of work. After seeing how much Jay and I enjoyed what we were doing, our girls certainly have been exposed to a positive view of work. I feel sorry for children who live in a household where a parent comes home at the end of the day and complains about how miserable he or she has been at work. What a sad message to send to young people, and what an unfortunate legacy to pass down to the next generation!

Because Jay and I were excited about The Pampered Chef, our daughters were excited too. As a result, they'd sometimes be the ones to initiate conversations about the business at the dinner table when Jay and I came prepared to discuss other subjects. Of course, there is nothing wrong with a family talking business at the table—as long as it's an agreeable subject for everyone.

I made sure we sat down at the dinner table as a family and ate good home-cooked meals often. Sure, there were occasions when I had a Kitchen Show and Jay was in charge. The girls actually looked forward to those times when the three of them were together. It was a time for father and daughters to bond. Many a night they'd talk Jay into popping in a TV dinner or taking them out for pizza! That was a real treat.

When I was gone doing a show, Jay never thought of himself as a babysitter. "I've heard other guys complain that they had to stay home and babysit," Jay says, "but I thought of it as being the parent in charge. Looking back, I was blessed to be able to have those times alone with the girls. I never thought of it as an inconvenience. They're my daughters too. When the three of us reminisce about those days, we have fond memories of good times together. All I have to do is say, 'Remember our quest for the perfect pizza?' and they immediately roll their eyes."

Kelley likes to tell the story about how she went to her father for help on a class science project. Her assignment was to compare the whitening qualities of different toothpastes. Jay took her to a dental laboratory to pick up real teeth that had previously been extracted. "It was kind of ghoulish," she laughs, "but my teacher thought it was definitely creative."

Jay and the girls are extremely close, and that is due in part to quality time they spent together when I was away.

4
MY EARLY YEARS
IN BUSINESS

The four bookings I got at my first Kitchen Show turned out to be not only wonderful learning experiences, but also a shot in the arm for my self-confidence. As I met people outside my own circle of friends and acquaintances at Kitchen Shows, I continued to book more of them. Jay told me some salespeople spend a disproportionate amount of time prospecting as opposed to actually selling. A novice stockbroker or insurance agent may make dozens of cold calls daily on the telephone soliciting sales leads. I was relieved to know this was one obstacle I would not encounter.

I quickly concluded that as long as I provided a high level of service and information and didn't apply high-pressure selling tactics, I could anticipate a steady flow of bookings. In fact, I expected my leads for bookings to grow exponentially. What really excited me was that my plan was working! My business was no longer a theory. I was performing a needed service that filled a void in the marketplace. I also had a flexible work schedule that

I controlled. I was able to work around my family's needs and remain a full-time mother. I could spend quality time with Julie and Kelley like a stay-at-home mom. I carpooled, went on field trips, baked cookies with my daughters after school, and I was making a little money, although that was secondary to having control of my time. I conducted Kitchen Shows in the evenings and on Saturday mornings when Jay was there to take over the parenting. My dream job enabled me to choose when I wanted to work, and I loved it. What working mother wouldn't?

Between October 15 and December 31 of that first year, I conducted eighteen Kitchen Shows that racked up $6,689.78 in gross sales, an average of $372 per show. That's a lot of shows to give in a two-month period. (With the Christmas holidays factored in, the month of December cuts off around the fifteenth.) I didn't anticipate giving eighteen shows in 1980, but at the same time I didn't want to say no to anyone who volunteered his or her support. So I overextended myself a bit in the beginning because I could sense momentum building, and I was not going to slow it down.

TIME MANAGEMENT

By the end of the year, I could see how my business could consume me—if I let it. Be resourceful, Doris, I told myself. Figure out how to work around the requirements of your family and your home and still give the business the time it needs.

How quickly I found out that operating a home-based business is not a typical nine-to-five, Monday-through-Friday job. If you let it, it's 24/7, 365 days a year. There was no end to the time you could put into it, because there's always something to do.

This meant I must pace myself and keep my priorities in order—family first, career second. I must never lose sight of why I started the business. My priorities had to be right to keep me from becoming a slave to my work. To let that happen would defeat my purpose in starting the business.

I need at least six hours of sleep and prefer seven. But if something has to be done or there's a deadline to meet, I'll stay up until the small hours. Besides, at night, without interruptions, I found I could be very productive. It was quite different during the day as I simultaneously did paperwork, worked in the storage room, ran loads through the washer and dryer, answered the phone, and baked cookies with Julie and Kelley. With the amount of running back and forth from the basement to the kitchen, I knew I'd never need a StairMaster. During the hours earmarked strictly for my daughters, my one-woman operation totally shut down.

I cut back on more than my sleep. For instance, television was one of my first sacrifices. Nielsen Media Research did studies in the 1980s that revealed adults averaged more than thirty hours of TV viewing each week. Just in this one area, a lot of wasted time could be put into my work. I also canceled several magazine subscriptions, and I practically stopped leisure reading. No more novels or lazy morning and weekend newspaper reading. My social life shrank too. For example, I used to play bridge with a group of women; although they met only monthly, I had to drop out. Eventually the pinochle club Jay and I were in had to go too.

I cherished my volunteer work, and it took me a while to realize I couldn't do everything I previously had done. For instance, at our church, I was particularly active in our women's society and on several committees. I headed the sewing booth for the church's major sale in the autumn, which meant hosting a group of women weekly at my house. As the Pampered Chef inventory built up, the lack of available space in the house meant we would have to meet elsewhere. This was an easy assessment compared to looking at my calendar and trying to figure out what fit and what didn't.

It was difficult to say no to requests for my time. Each painful decision made me feel guilty because there are many wonderful causes to support. This is especially true around the Christmas holidays. Just the same, I couldn't do everything. I found myself looking at my calendar for things to cut back on without doing away with what truly mattered to me. Each of us must set boundaries, I told myself, and around the holidays, my family clearly came first.

At one women's society board meeting, I remember sadly thinking, "I don't have time for this anymore." I resigned with regret, because I enjoyed these activities, and in particular, working with such good people. I volunteered to do what I could from home. I made phone calls for church and school projects and some fund-raising calls, but eventually I had to eliminate these activities too. The demands of the business were so seductive, they took precedence over practically everything except the children's activities. Ultimately, they were my primary goal—I refused to make sacrifices that would interfere with my time with them, especially their school-related activities.

THE SECOND KITCHEN CONSULTANT

After a few shows, I intuitively knew the day would come when I would have to hire other Kitchen Consultants. My business was simply too good to keep to myself. I realized other working mothers could share the advantages I derived from flexible hours.

Jay pointed out a big advantage in having a sales force. "It's leverage," he emphasized. "With a sales force your income does not depend entirely on your ability to get out of bed and go to work every day. You'll benefit from the efforts of others in addition to your own efforts. This way, Doris, you'll have income even when you're home sick or away on vacation."

"Someday down the road I'd like to do that," I agreed. "But right now I don't feel comfortable taking on added responsibility."

"You're doing just fine, dear, at what you're doing."

Meanwhile, I was content being the world's one and only Kitchen Consultant. I loved giving Kitchen Shows, and I was perfectly happy giving them to small groups of women a few times a week, earning money that would go toward my daughters' college education. That was my initial goal, and knowing it was doable was a great source of satisfaction. At the same time, I loved demonstrating that my products were functional, time-efficient tools. I was enjoying my new business.

Then one night in May 1981, the inevitable happened. As I was packing up at the end of a show, a woman approached me, Kim Bass, a twenty-five-year-old mother of two. "Are you looking for anyone else to help you with this?" she stammered.

Her question took me by surprise. Kim continued, "I think I could do this, Doris. I think it would work for me."

I anticipated that a time would come when I would want to build a sales organization, but the business was only nine months old and I wasn't sure that this was the right time. Was I far enough into it, or did I understand it well enough to take on other people? "Let me think about it," I said. "Give me your phone number and I'll call you in a day or two."

Driving home that night, I kept thinking about Kim Bass. By coincidence her background was similar to mine—she too was trained as a home economist. I knew she was an intelligent, responsible person. A lot of other people could have asked me and I would have wondered whether they could do it. But with Kim, I had no doubt she was well qualified. If I had been looking for someone, she would have been the ultimate candidate. Still, I was unsure about what to do. I didn't know how to pay her, because at the time, I was working without compensation myself. How would I set up a commission schedule? But as I thought about it, I was confident Jay could figure it out. Another potential problem was that I wasn't sure how to train someone. In the back of my mind, I had envisioned having a good solid year under my belt before I'd be ready to grow the business by adding on other people. I raced home that night, eager to get some feedback from Jay.

When I got home, Jay was watching Johnny Carson. He turned down the sound and helped me carry in my crates. As always, he immediately started asking questions: "Did you get a nice turnout?" "What did you sell?" "Get many bookings?" "Come up with any new ideas?"

I answered his questions, then dropped my bombshell. "Something else happened this time, Jay." I told him all about Kim and added, "She's the ideal candidate, isn't she?"

"Yes. She sounds great."

I explained my concerns about determining her compensation. Jay said, "No problem. I've been giving this some thought, and I'll devise something that should work."

"I've thought about how I'd train her," I said. "She's bright and knows her way around the kitchen, so if I take her with me to watch a few shows . . ."

"Right, and review the inventory and price list with her," Jay volunteered.

"What I'm most concerned about," I added, "is with our light inventory, whether we have the resources to make this work. Every time I go out to do a show, I check the inventory downstairs so I know exactly what's down there. I know if there's two stones or ten stones on the shelves, and that's what I sell. And based on what we've got, I also know to say to a customer, 'It's going to take an extra week or two before I can get this to you.' "

"Yes, you're familiar with what's in stock," he replied. "And Kim won't know."

"That's my biggest concern. I know how to manage the inventory as a one-woman operation, but how will I know what to do when two of us are giving Kitchen Shows?"

"We'll make it work, Doris," Jay said. "We may have to carry a slightly bigger inventory, but since everything you earn has been put into buying more products, we can handle it."

I looked at Jay and shrugged my shoulders.

"Let's give it a try," he said.

Excited, I called Kim and said, "Let's get together and talk about how we can get you into this."

When we met, I showed her what she would sell, and told her what she'd get paid. I was candid with her about the commission schedule. "We'll try this but we're not sure it's going to work. But this is what we'll start with."

I held my breath until she nodded. "Sounds okay with me. I'm looking forward to working with you."

We had to make four or five adjustments to the commission schedule during the first six months until it worked for both of us.

Kim accompanied me to two shows. With her background, everything I did came naturally to her. She started off with a bang. But it caused me to wonder, does it take a home economist to succeed in this business? Can others be just as effective? If only a home economist could do what Kim and I were doing, our future recruiting efforts would be limited.

I discovered an unexpected bonus in not being the sole Kitchen Consultant for The Pampered Chef. I had somebody to share experiences with! In this respect Kim was like a partner. We shared our successes, discussed our failures, and cross-pollinated ideas on how to do things better. Suddenly, there was someone else who faced the same challenges I did!

Conveniently, Kim lived only a mile away. We could easily get together for brief chats and she could stop by to pick up products. Although we shared some acquaintances—neighbors and members of our church—Kim had her own circle of friends consisting of former classmates and her husband's co-workers. This was a great boon to the business because Kim traveled to different areas throughout Chicago, spreading the word about our little-known but growing Pampered Chef.

My concern about managing our inventory with another person on board turned out to be baseless. Because we communicated so beautifully, the problem never arose. When Kim booked evening shows, she'd call or stop by my house earlier in the day to review the products in inventory.

"This is what we both have," I'd tell her. "Tell me what you'll be showing, and I'll show something else."

On nights we both had shows, and inventory was limited,

we'd each agree to sell no more than a set number of a specific product. On nights when she booked a show and I didn't, the entire inventory was hers to draw on, and vice versa. Fortunately, a few suppliers were located in Chicago, such as our stoneware wholesaler. Whenever necessary, I could drive to the supplier's warehouse to make a pickup. By keeping on top of the state of our inventory, we reduced the likelihood of selling products not stocked in our basement.

Seeing how well Kim was working out, I started recruiting and training other women to be Kitchen Consultants. Between May and October, our sales force of two grew to ten. I continued to give Kitchen Shows myself, and now had the added responsibility of managing a number of other people. These were exciting times for me. I enjoyed seeing other women who, like me, wanted work with flexible hours so they could schedule their work around their families' needs. I quickly realized a good Kitchen Consultant didn't need a home economics background, or even a background in teaching. I was thrilled to discover that all kinds of people could succeed in this line of work. There were only two prerequisites: the person must have access to a car and she must have a circle of friends. Fortunately, most people I met fit these criteria.

I also learned early on that our products appealed to a wide variety of consumers—even to those who didn't cook, or who claimed they didn't cook. I vividly remember at early Kitchen Shows hearing people who were just arriving saying, "I don't know what I'm doing here. I never cook." When I first heard such comments, I was discouraged, thinking I was in for a tough evening, a poor reception from a group of people who didn't cook. It didn't take me long to realize that some of these people could be good customers. As it turned out, those who didn't cook had very little of what I was selling in their kitchens, so many of my products appealed to them. I learned a valuable lesson from these shows—there is almost no such thing as a bad customer for our business. Those who love to cook became totally immersed at our shows. Those who didn't were happy to discover that we could help them with this task they didn't like. What's more, I recognized we appealed to different age groups as well as different socioeconomic groups. Our cooking tools interested a wide range from young mothers at home with small children to empty nesters. In terms of finding Consultants, we attracted seekers of both full-time and part-time employment.

We were very careful not to recruit other companies' salespeople. I thought someone who was leaving one organization to sell for another was a poor prospect for us. First, I thought that because we were so new and small, we didn't have resources to match their compensation and incentive programs. Second, I didn't want people who were dissatisfied with where they came from coming to us with a lot of baggage that could negatively impact our small organization.

NO MORE SATURDAY DELIVERIES!

On Saturday mornings, I loaded up my Plymouth Volare, a compact sedan, and Jay would do the same with his car. Then we'd go our separate ways, making deliveries. Needless to say, these deliveries were time-consuming and sometimes took up a good part of our day. Months later, Jay and I followed a similar routine, delivering merchandise to our Kitchen Consultants, who in turn dropped off packages at their hosts' residences. To speed up the process, Kitchen Consultants sometimes stopped by our house during the week to pick up merchandise.

As our Saturday deliveries grew, we realized this wasn't the most productive use of our time.

"This has to stop," Jay complained. "We've got to start using UPS for deliveries."

"I know you're right," I said. "But I do enjoy the time I spend talking to our customers. Visiting with them helps me provide them high-quality service. I hate to give up getting that feedback."

"We've got ten other Kitchen Consultants to give us feedback," Jay said. "I'm calling UPS to set up an account."

I knew Jay was right, although, I must confess, I consented with ambivalence. But I knew that for the business to grow, it was the right decision. Those personal deliveries put considerable constraints on future expansion. Geographically, there was a distance barrier that limited how far we could deliver orders.

"The UPS charges will add an extra cost to what our customers buy from us," I reminded Jay.

"Tell them at the Kitchen Show that there will be a UPS charge," Jay said matter-of-factly. "I don't think they'll mind. People are used to paying shipping charges. They do it all the time when they buy from a mail order catalog. And they pay for shipping when a retail store sends merchandise to them. It shouldn't affect our business."

We started shipping via UPS in late 1981, adding a shipping fee to the order form. Jay was right—there were very few complaints.

Once we had a UPS account, we called them whenever we had to ship something. We lived in a residential neighborhood where it was unusual for anyone to send out many packages. In the beginning, our pickups weren't big enough for anyone at UPS to take notice. There were more incoming packages from suppliers than what we shipped out. Pretty soon, however, the UPS drivers began to get curious. What was the small Victorian house at 1449 Thatcher Avenue?

Soon the daily pickups averaged ten, twenty, and thirty packages. To our good fortune, the UPS hub was nearby and we were the last stop on the route at the end of the day before the driver headed home. This meant we had all day to put orders together. It also meant we were the first stop of the day when the UPS driver started his delivery route. Because the packages arrived intermittently, our packages were spread out among other packages throughout the truck. This caused drivers to have to make several stops at our house in a single day. UPS is very good at what it does; when these inefficiencies became apparent, they loaded the truck with all of our packages in the back of the truck, making ours the first stop to be unloaded. This worked beautifully for us. We received incoming shipments early in the morning and we had the entire day to unpack the merchandise and put it in outbound orders that were picked up in the late afternoon.

As the number of our outgoing packages increased, however, it became increasingly difficult for UPS to pick them up. We were not a typical business account—our tall but small Victorian house had a narrow driveway that even the smaller UPS trucks had difficulty navigating. There was only about a foot of clearance, and from inside the truck it seemed like only a few inches. To make matters worse, the driver had to unload the truck, come in a side entrance, and then go down a narrow basement staircase with an armful of boxes. The entrance had a low overhang, and the staircase had an even lower ceiling. Big, strapping drivers could barely squeeze through, and I'd hear occasional expletives when someone would bump his head. Although conditions weren't ideal, the UPS drivers were always courteous and friendly. We couldn't have been their favorite stop on the route, but they didn't complain.

Over time, we became friendly with the drivers. One driver, Steve Yoshikane, an Asian American, stands out as particularly memorable; a short, slightly built man, he was a workhorse who maneuvered the stairs with ease, springing back and forth from the truck to the basement and never once hitting his head on the low overhang.

Having the UPS truck pull in to make a delivery was always one of the day's highlights for me. It was particularly exciting when new merchandise arrived that hadn't previously been part of our line.

River Forest is an upscale neighborhood. Typically such a community has zoning restrictions, in addition to neighbors likely to complain about trucks pulling in and out. Fortunately, we lived across the street from a forest preserve, where there was no one to complain.

GRAND CENTRAL STATION

By the end of 1981, our first full year in business, we had twelve Kitchen Consultants and revenues totaling $67,000. At about $1,000 a week, we were still a very small company that had yet to stretch its wings.

The Pampered Chef remained a family affair. I did the buying, testing, and selling of all our products. I also created recipes and recruited and trained Kitchen Consultants. Jay was in charge of financing, warehousing, packing, and shipping. Operating a start-up business out of our house meant nobody had a title. I too helped in warehousing, packing, and shipping.

When something has to be done in a small business, you can't say, "That's not my job." You just do it. For instance when a UPS shipment arrived in the morning with merchandise that had to be repackaged and shipped out by late afternoon, I didn't have the option of saying, "Oh, that's Jay's responsibility." At the time, Jay was working for Lien Chemical Company; he wouldn't be home from his "real" job until long after the UPS pickup truck was gone. So unpacking and repacking became my job. Even Julie and Kelley pitched in. One of their earliest assignments was stamping bags with the Pampered Chef logo.

In the beginning, we did all the work ourselves. Back then, we didn't think much of it. But in retrospect, I'm astonished how much there was to do: design the paperwork, create an accounting system, coach Kitchen Consultants. On those evenings when I was giving a show, after Julie and Kelley were asleep, Jay would sometimes go down to the basement to pack orders, take inventory, or break down boxes to make room for the next day's arrival of UPS packages. Sometimes it seemed as if his one mission in life was to make more space out of our cramped basement. On occasion I complained that he was too organized, to which he responded, "It's impossible to be too organized."

Consumed with the business, Jay would frequently disappear into the basement after dinner and stay there until after midnight. Some Saturdays, he'd be down there at nine in the morning and work until the midafternoon. Of course those were my times with the girls.

It wasn't too long before we had to hire people to work on an as-needed basis. Fortunately, there were always people who wanted to work part time; we always had a large pool of labor from which to draw. Most were women I knew from church who wanted to make some extra money while their children were in school. For instance, Dianne Beck, a longtime friend of ours. Her husband Bob had gone to high school with Jay and me. Prior to starting the business, I used to drop Julie off at Dianne's house when I needed a free morning, and she'd drop her son at my house. With two boys who were roughly the same age as our girls, Dianne wanted a ten-to-two job to give her time to be with her children before and after school. While her older son was in school, she would leave her younger boy with her mother, who lived in River Forest. A very responsible person, Dianne told me upfront that she wouldn't commit to a job she couldn't fulfill. She was one of the most reliable persons I have ever known. A former legal secretary, she worked for us as a jack-of-all-trades, excelling at bookkeeping, order processing, and order packing.

Linda Rock was recommended to me by the sister of a friend. Feeling burned out from her teaching career, Linda was our first full-time employee. Her work began with typing letters and helping create newsletters, but perhaps due to her teaching background, Linda was especially good at training new people. She worked with us for about eighteen months. Eventually, however, Linda realized that her heart was still in teaching and she returned to teaching full time.

When I realized Linda was leaving, I hired, at Jay's recommendation, Joan Tomasello, who had worked with Jay for ten years at Lien Chemical, to replace her. Joan became our first office manager. While Linda's work had focused more on training, Joan hired, trained, and managed our internal people. She was also instrumental in setting up our office and warehouse procedures.

Altogether, a dozen or so women I knew from church and the local community worked part time for us. When school was out, the part-time women went home to be with their children, and were replaced by a second shift: kids looking for a few work hours after school. Being home-based, we were particular about who worked for us. One good source for part-time help was the Collins family, three houses down the street from us. Their three kids, Logan, Michelle, and Jenny, each started babysitting for us, and then ended up working for us after school and on weekends. Like a lot of kids in the neighborhood, the Collins kids continued to work off and on for us even when they were in college, including summers and holiday seasons.

By far the busiest day of the month was the Saturday I conducted our monthly sales meeting. Since all our consultants were located in the Chicago area, our entire sales force was invited to my house. I spent a major portion of the Friday before it getting ready—as well as preparing a delicious brunch for all who attended. I prided myself on entertaining in my home, and I went all out to make sure my Kitchen Consultants received VIP treatment. Like a Kitchen Show, part of the Saturday meeting revolved around what I prepared in my kitchen—always something that could be duplicated and that would demonstrate our kitchen tools.

Upon arrival, the consultants turned in their supply orders and Dianne, working in the basement, filled them, getting them packed and ready to go by the end of the meeting. Later on, to expedite the process, their orders were often submitted earlier in the week. While other staff members worked in the basement, our sales force assembled around the dining room table. Each consultant posted her upcoming Kitchen Shows, enabling us to project how much inventory to order.

These Saturday get-togethers were fun—we had a good time—but we also got right down to business. I didn't want to take anyone away from her family on a Saturday morning without making sure she came away with something that would benefit her career. Topics ranged from how to make a good presentation to tips on how to use items from our product line. When a new kitchen tool was introduced, we always attached instructions on how to apply it in an accompanying recipe. Note-taking abounded as everyone related what worked best for her during a Kitchen Show. Between Dianne in the basement and my group upstairs, our small Victorian house was filled with so much energy you could feel it. Not to mention people. Grand Central Station had nothing on us.

TIME TO LEAVE HOME

Our sales organization continued to expand, and by the end of 1982 we had twenty-five Kitchen Consultants. Our product line increased to ninety kitchen tools and our revenues doubled to $100,000. Sales doubled again the following year. By the end of 1984, our revenues totaled $499,000. From day one, my makeshift office and storage area created a very tight fit in our four-hundred-square-foot basement. By 1984, with three desks crammed downstairs, it became even tighter. Poor Linda's desk was next to the furnace. Inventory was stacked floor to ceiling. Our garage was also filled with inventory, stacked on pallets to prevent mildew. As in the basement, Jay had to maneuver his way through it by walking sideways. He used to brag about keeping himself in good condition by carrying packages from garage to basement. It used to upset my father, an auto mechanic, because we parked our cars in the driveway when we had "a perfectly good garage."

The basement was already overcrowded with Dianne, Linda,

and me. So you can imagine what it was like during our busiest time of the year—the long Thanksgiving weekend, when eight to ten part-time high school kids on break came for a hectic four-day stretch. With Christmas right around the corner, we needed all our part-timers to get packages out the door. Although our Pampered Chef products sold well throughout the year, our sales peaked in October through early December for Christmas and holiday cooking. It didn't matter that there were too many people to fit into our 1,700-square-foot house—we needed every able body to pitch in. Anyone who wanted to work was invited to come in Thursday evening after finishing Thanksgiving dinner. The next morning we started at dawn. Quitting time was 9:00 p.m., and it was this way day and night until the week before Christmas.

The UPS pickup truck that stopped by the house late Wednesday afternoon before Thanksgiving was the last one until the following Monday afternoon. This meant we worked for the next five days getting packages ready to be shipped for a late Monday afternoon UPS pickup. Under normal circumstances, boxing, labeling, and organizing everything for that Monday's late UPS pickup was an enormous task. To compound matters, everyone kept getting in one another's way. We quickly ran out of physical space in the basement. There was never enough room; now there simply wasn't any room. Our overcrowded basement forced the accounting people to move upstairs, doing their work on the dining room table. People in the living room stamped labels on paper bags. Other workers handwrote shipping labels and attached them to boxes that others had securely packaged and taped. To an outsider, it looked like mass confusion!

By Sunday the living room was filled and packages were being stacked from floor to ceiling in the dining room. By Monday, boxes were stacked on both sides of the stairs going to the second floor. Only by walking sideways was I able to pass through.

That Monday, Jay and I stared in disbelief at what had happened to the interior of our house. "Never again," I said to Jay. "We can't go through another Thanksgiving like this."

"Amen," he sighed.

Seeing our house besieged with ceiling-high stacks of boxes was a defining moment; we needed to get this thing out of our house. That week we started looking for a commercial building.

A vacant 2,500-square-foot building that had housed an insurance agency had been on the market for one week. Located at 340 Lathrop Avenue in a River Forest commercial area, it was only two miles from our house. Jay and I thought it would be ideal for our business. Jay's father, a real estate attorney, guided us through the entire buying process. At $121,000, the building was ours. The sale happened so fast I didn't have time to worry about it. It was our company's first long-term commitment.

The two-story building had an apartment upstairs, and the rental income it brought in helped us to make the mortgage payments. The first floor had several small offices in the front and sufficient room in the back for packing, shipping, and storage. We could lay inventory out in the order of our price list so it could be picked more efficiently. We even had a legitimate place for regular truck lines to stop. There was a garage, as well, but the upstairs tenant's lease gave him the right to use it; only later when he moved out did we move our offices upstairs and use the garage for inventory. With 2,500 square feet, it seemed as if we'd never have to move again.

When the business moved to 340 Lathrop Avenue, I exclaimed to Jay, "We've got our house back!" Once again the girls had a basement they could play in, particularly when their friends visited. Every day their school bus dropped Julie and Kelley off at our building after school. When they arrived, my day at the office ended.

It took a while for me to make the adjustment to working outside the home. I was used to running downstairs to squeeze in a little extra work in the evenings; no longer could I multitask while I had a full load in the washer and dryer. In the beginning, I found myself running over to the office to do something "urgent." Over time I learned to take what was "urgent" home in a briefcase. I also became better organized and improved my time management skills. I discovered that when I worked in my home with no time constraints, I had no pressure to get something done. With an office to go to, I had to wrap up things before day's end. Then too, at the office, there were fewer distractions— no personal chores such as cooking, laundry, yard work, and so on. Plus, I had people there who screened phone calls and solicitors. This too allowed me to make better use of my time.

Once The Pampered Chef was out of the house, we felt more like a real business. We had real business hours. Vendors treated us differently too—they took us more seriously. For one thing, I don't think they worried as much about whether we had enough money to pay our bills. Working out of the house left some with the impression that our company was a bit shaky. And while our part-time workers rarely complained about working in our home, they also enjoyed the change. "When the business was in your home," one told me, "at times I felt I was intruding on your family's privacy."

THE SHOPPING CART CONVOY

After running our business from the basement of our small home, our building seemed more than spacious. The first floor was as large as our entire house! Perhaps nobody was more elated than the UPS drivers. No more carrying packages up and down our basement stairs! Nor did they have to maneuver their trucks up and down our driveway. In addition, larger trucks could now make deliveries at our building, because there was an alley behind the building where they could park.

Still, there was room for improvement. We didn't have a loading dock, for example. As our volume increased, large containers could be dropped off behind the building; but without a loading dock, it was quite laborious to unload trucks, disassemble large containers, and carry merchandise inside.

As our daily shipments grew larger, we had to find a way to ease the burden on our staff. It was tiring to carry packages to the warehouse area, go back to the alley, and repeat this procedure until everything was brought inside. Jay finally came up with a relatively simple solution that greatly reduced this exhausting task. We bought used shopping carts to wheel the packages in. Not only did this reduce lifting, it also meant fewer trips back and forth. In his search to save time and reduce labor costs, Jay even devised a peculiar contraption using skate rollers to wheel boxes from the truck to the storage area.

THE IMPACT ON THE BOTTOM LINE

Right from the start of The Pampered Chef, I was conditioned to be very tight with the penny when I went to the Merchandise Mart. Even though I was buying in small quantities, I always tried to negotiate a discounted price that matched what was paid by customers who were volume buyers. With only $3,000 in the kitty, I had to be ultrafrugal. This good discipline paid off when we became a larger company.

With our new business location, for the first time we took on many new business expenses. Now we had mortgage payments, real estate taxes, utilities, janitorial services, and business insurance.

Worried that our new overhead would burden us, we moved into the building without a bit of remodeling. We didn't even paint the walls or replace the carpeting. We took our old furniture with us and thought nothing of it. We always looked for a bargain, and if we could buy something used, we did, including furniture, filing cabinets, shelving, and office equipment.

My philosophy was that if something wasn't really necessary, we didn't spend money on it. We confined our spending to what was essential. This is good advice even for a mature business; for a hole-in-the-wall company, it's the only option. With a limited budget, we could afford to buy only what was absolutely mandatory. We worked just as effectively with a used desk as a fancy new one. We didn't rent space at a prestigious address, because our business didn't require it. Nor did we advertise that we had moved. Why? Again, it wouldn't have made any difference.

If you're planning on starting a new business, you need a clear understanding about what you really plan to do. Knowing that will let you determine where you should be putting your money. In the retail business, it's location, location, location. In a high-profile business, image is important. For instance, in a supermarket, the attractiveness of a box of cereal or bag of potato chips might induce consumers to buy an off-brand product. A retailer is apt to pay a high premium to design product packaging. Packaging can even be the tie-breaker for the shopper undecided whether to buy one brand-name product or another. In our business, however, packaging is strictly protection for shipping our products. We differ from a retailer in that we sell our products by demonstrating how to use them when they are out of the box. For this reason, we don't put a lot of money or design into artful packaging, because it doesn't impact our bottom line.

I remember when we bought our first copying machine. We held off buying one until our volume of copying finally justified the purchase. Previously, we used carbon paper, or when necessary we'd go to a local print shop or my father-in-law's nearby law office to make copies. Once the decision was made, I called a copying machine salesman whom Jay had previously worked with, and he came out to do a demonstration. The salesman wheeled in a copier with all the bells and whistles, set it up, and gave his demonstration. It was a high-speed model that collated pages. My secretary and I were in awe.

He started to write up an order form. When he was finished, he said, "Sign here and I'll have a new model delivered by early next week."

But when I took one look at the monthly payment, I said, "It's far more than we can afford. What less expensive models can you show us?"

He agreed to come back the following day with another model. Again, he gave a demonstration. "This machine is brand-new, so you can just keep this one," he said, filling out the order form.

"It's still too expensive," I told him. "I'm just going to have to think about it. I've got to figure out if we can do our newsletter on it, or if we still have to have it copied outside."

Two calls later, he presented the least expensive model in his line to us. It was priced right and affordable. I still had some concerns about its reliability—would it work when we needed it for a pressing job? The salesman assured me my worry was unwarranted.

"Okay, let's talk about what kind of deal you can give us on a maintenance contract," I said.

We went back and forth on the contract; it was only when he agreed to give us a six-month supply of copying paper that I signed the order form. We had to be the most difficult sale of his career!

IN SEARCH OF EXCELLENT PRODUCTS

Ever since my first trip to the Merchandise Mart, I've been on a constant search for new products. We're never satisfied with the status quo. We refuse to rest on our laurels.

With each product, I assess whether it meets my requirements both functionally and qualitatively. To this day, every time I pick up a magazine such as *Better Homes and Gardens* or *House Beautiful,* I look for new kitchenware. The catalogs that sell housewares and gift products, I read cover to cover. I read the trade magazines. I constantly shop in hardware stores, gift shops, and department stores. I can't help it. I can't walk through a shopping mall without making a stop or two, hoping I might come across a new find. Years ago, the National Association of Housewares Manufacturers held two shows a year at McCormick Place in Chicago, in January and July. Early on, these shows were tremendous conveniences to us. As a start-up company, I could not have afforded to visit these trade shows if it required traveling a long distance. It was my good fortune that these shows were held in my own backyard. Larger companies dispatched their people on buying trips to Europe and the Far East. I couldn't even afford to go to New York, let alone a trip abroad. (Today, of course, it's a different story; our buyers travel all over the world in a constant quest to find something new and exciting.)

Improving our product line is an ongoing process. A product might be dropped from the line because it doesn't sell well; at other times, a good seller is eliminated because of customer complaints. We are constantly dropping products and adding new ones.

By no means are all our products winners. One early loser was a steamed pudding mold. Shaped like a small lunch bucket, it had a fluted bottom with a top that could be tightly clamped on. It formed a fancy steamed pudding that could be taken out of the container and served during the holidays. I thought it was clever and interesting and expected it to be a big seller. I placed an initial order for two units but found no buyers for them. Ultimately, I kept one for my kitchen and the other is somewhere in our company archives. Why didn't it sell? I realized after the fact that it took too much time to be demonstrated at a Kitchen Show. It also failed to meet one of our most important criteria— saving time in the kitchen. Of course some products take too much time to demonstrate but can be sold with an explanation, such as our perennial top seller, the pizza stone. But that wasn't the case with the steamed pudding mold.

Early on we introduced some holiday aprons and potholders that I thought were interesting and attractive. But I soon discovered that such holiday items didn't work well for us. To our customers, The Pampered Chef stood for products that saved time in the kitchen. We also had a problem offering stylish products because we were unable to offer a full array of fashion and colors. As a result, only recently, in our twenty-fifth year, have we started to offer color in our line.

In my continual search for new products, I was always reading the trendy eight-page food section that used to appear in the Thursday edition of the *Chicago Tribune*. In one November letter to the editor, a reader wrote that she loved the Norwegian deep-fried pastry called Fattigman that her mother made during the Christmas season. "My mother had a Fattigman cutter; however, I am unable to find one in any of the kitchen stores in Chicago. I loved those Fattigmans and would like to make them for my family. Can you advise me where to buy a Fattigman cutter?"

After reading the letter I checked with a supplier of Swedish and Norwegian products, and sure enough, they carried a Fattigman cutter. I promptly notified the editor at the newspaper that The Pampered Chef had one in our line. I stated the price and gave our address and phone number for anyone who wanted to buy one from us. The following Thursday's *Trib* food section included a comment from the editor: "About that Fattigman cutter a reader asked about—The Pampered Chef has them." The article gave our address and phone number along with the cutter's $8 price tag. To be ready for the onslaught of orders we anticipated, we purchased fifty units. We ended up selling ten of them. While the Fattigman cutter was an excellent product, once again it was time-consuming to use and it could not be easily demonstrated at a Kitchen Show. Getting stuck with forty units was a costly lesson to our fledgling company.

Several whimsical products in our line also had to be discontinued. For instance, we had a Pig Wand: a cotton-stuffed little pig's face on the end of a rod. One wave of the wand over food would instantly remove all calories. It was strictly a novelty item that sold well at shows as a gag gift. A woman made them in her home. But when we increased our orders, she was unable to supply us with the quantity we needed. And the woman didn't want to manufacture them on a large scale. As a result, we stopped selling Pig Wands. Admittedly, it was gimmicky, and wouldn't have had much staying power in the long term.

Other early products that bombed? We had a self-watering Christmas tree ornament. (Jay personally came up with this concoction.) Water was poured into a bell-shaped container that hung from a branch and it flowed down to the base to water the tree. And there was our six-in-one utility tool, a hammer with a brass handle that unscrewed and contained five different screwdriver sizes. While this was a handy gadget to fix little things, it could be purchased anywhere—hardware stores, grocery stores, counters at gasoline stations—at far less cost. We can't compete with mass merchandisers that work on low margins. Then there was the needlepoint sign to be hung on the dishwater that said "clean" or "dirty." And the green plastic onion goggles that protected your eyes from tearing.

One big-selling item that we discontinued was the Super Swat, a flyswatter equipped with tweezers that fit into a slot on its handle. The tweezers are used to pick up the dead fly. Practical in the kitchen and handy on picnics, it was well received by our customers. But not long after the flyswatter's introduction, we decided we would accompany every product with a recipe. Because we couldn't do that with the swatter, we took it out of the line. Immediately afterward, we heard from a lot of our Kitchen Consultants, who told us, "I used it as a funny product to talk about at the end of my presentation. I'd say, 'If you don't cook, I still have something you can use. This Super Swat.' "

As a joke at one of our sales conferences, Jay passed out self-addressed, post-paid postcards to everyone he talked to. In bold print it said, BRING BACK THE SUPER SWAT. I couldn't get over how many of those cards we received. Thousands—even from people who didn't attend the conference. So by popular demand, the Super Swat was revived, and its sales remained brisk for several years.

GROWING BY LEAPS AND BOUNDS

By the end of 1985, our sales totaled $592,700 and our product line had jumped to 162 products. Our sales force had increased to thirty-two Kitchen Consultants. Around this time, I was gradually reducing the number of Kitchen Shows I personally did. Of course there was a time when my sales accounted for all of our company's revenues. And even with several dozen Kitchen Consultants, I was responsible for about half of our total sales. So removing myself from the field was a difficult transition. But it was one I felt was necessary to grow the company. Still, I enjoyed doing Kitchen Shows, and I liked the one-on-one interaction with customers, so I continued to do the shows for my friends, for training, and when I recruited out of town.

Two years after our move to the new location, we were nearing the million-dollar mark in revenues, a major milestone.

My mother was always supportive of everything my sisters and I did, but in the early years of my business, I think she would have preferred me to have a job in teaching or home economics. Although she never came out and said anything negative, one time she asked, "Are you still doing that Pampered Chef thing?" I answered, "Gosh, Mom! It's as if someone asked, 'Do you still have your child?' "

When the tenant's lease on the second-floor apartment terminated, we moved our offices upstairs and used the entire first floor for operations. In 1989 we bought the building next door. While the new building had the same amount of office space, it had four times as much warehouse and distribution area. So we sold our first building at a small profit and applied the proceeds to what seemed like more space than we could ever use.

And our product line kept growing! To promote our brand name, we started repackaging products by putting them in plastic bags and stapling a header with the Pampered Chef name on it. In the early years, we carried many recognizable brand-name products. We sold Leifheit, a wonderful German brand of houseware products such as choppers, slicers, and cookie presses. We also sold Zyliss, a fine Swiss line that had similar products. In the beginning, I merely selected the best available products to sell. However, as we grew bigger and The Pampered Chef became an important customer to our vendors and suppliers, we were able to give input to manufacturers on what we expected of a particular product. Still later, we became big enough to request a manufacturer to custom-make products to meet our specifications. Gradually, over the years, fewer and fewer products bore the manufacturer's name; instead, they had our name. Of course, we had to place sizable orders to justify this treatment from a manufacturer. Much later, we did sufficient volume with certain manufacturers that they agreed to make specific products exclusively for The Pampered Chef.

A GUTSY MOVE

In 1986, Jay left Lien Chemical after receiving an attractive offer from Marian Joy Rehabilitation Hospital, a well-regarded medical institution in the Chicago area that had plans to establish satellite medical centers throughout northern Illinois. Jay was responsible for heading up their expansion program. A year later, when the hospital decided to move in a different direction, Jay resigned.

Meanwhile, with sales at $1 million and growing, The Pampered Chef was in need of a qualified executive who could take charge of our warehousing and distribution. With a staff of part-time people, the company was not operating at the kind of professional level that would take us forward. I could read the handwriting on the wall. We had to hire a top person to head the operational side of our business. I knew we had to act quickly before things got out of control, causing our company to grind to a halt.

We desperately needed Jay's services. So Jay agreed to work on our operationals on an interim basis while job searching. But I could only afford to pay him a $10,000 annual salary, considerably less than his former wages. And I still was not drawing a salary from the company. So we had to tighten our belts to make ends meet.

After Jay spent a few months on the job, we confirmed something that we were never quite sure about before—the two of us could work well together. Believe me, this is something a husband and wife never know for sure until they attempt it full time with no other source of income. When we realized how valuable Jay was to the business, he agreed to stop his job search and work full time for The Pampered Chef.

It was a gutsy move, because we didn't have money put away for the girls' college educations, and there was no way we could save money on the meager salary Jay was paid by our company. And of course there was no guarantee that our company would succeed and be able to provide our family with an adequate income. Talk about putting all of our eggs in one basket!

Jay's passion has always been the back end of the business, operations. He thrives on doing warehouse design, and as we grew, he started doing the computer systems. The sales side of the business, which I handled, is what's glamorous and gets most of the attention. Our Kitchen Consultants often took what Jay did for granted; it's something that they expected to happen. This is particularly true when everything is running smoothly. As a consequence, he didn't receive the kudos he deserved for setting up the operations and financial end of the company. We both know, however, that I couldn't have made The Pampered Chef the success it is without him.

Eventually it came time to incorporate the company. Jay and I met with his father, who handled the paperwork. Just before we filed our articles of incorporation, the three of us met in our dining room. "Everything is ready," his father said. "The only thing I need to fill out on this form is what the stock split should be. Do you want it fifty-fifty?"

"No," Jay answered. "Doris gets fifty-one percent and I get forty-nine percent."

"Why?" his father asked.

"I once worked for a very smart gentleman, an executive who came out of Continental Bank," Jay said, "and he always said that you never do a fifty-fifty deal. Somebody has to make that decision. And Doris is in charge of this company. She gets fifty-one percent."

As husband and wife, Jay and I are life partners; for me it has been a partnership made in heaven.

5
BUILDING THE
SALES ORGANIZATION

Back in 1980, when I was the only Kitchen Consultant, I couldn't have imagined the sales organization we have today. I wasn't even sure there would be a second Kitchen Consultant.

Today, our sales organization is the company's crown jewel. In those early days, we were based primarily in the suburbs of Chicago. Today, the company is represented in all fifty states, as well as in Canada, Great Britain, and Germany. But back in 1981, a strong snowstorm hitting Chicago could shut us down. There were nights when every Kitchen Show was canceled due to poor weather conditions! Many a night I drove through ice and snow to a hostess's house and no one showed up. In those days we didn't have cell phones, so it wasn't possible to call off a show at the last minute. Now we're spread out in so many different directions, poor weather conditions can no longer put us totally out of commission.

Remember the six heavy wooden crates I struggled with at my first Kitchen Show? Well, today's Kitchen Consultant carries only one, and our current version is considerably lighter than the original. In the beginning, a lumber store cut pieces of wood for our crates, which Jay then assembled. Later on we bought prefabricated crates from another lumber company.

One reason a Kitchen Consultant carries only one crate is that we now have full-line catalogs that eloquently present our products. In 1980 we had a single sheet of paper with our entire product line printed on both sides. Today the line is presented by demonstrating actual products *and* by showing customers catalogs with beautiful photographs. For instance, a pizza stone doesn't have to be brought to a show, unless, of course, the consultant plans to prepare a recipe with it. Then it is necessary to show only one piece of stoneware; a prospective buyer can see other stones in various shapes by viewing catalog photographs.

The evolution of the sales catalog from mimeographed sheets to pages of full-color photographs parallels how the entire business grew during those early years. The Pampered Chef was the furthest thing from an overnight success story. After we hired Kim, our second Kitchen Consultant, others slowly joined, and I continued to sell side by side with them. I was always experimenting, tinkering with how much to charge for the products, how much to pay Kitchen Consultants, and what to sell. At first, by trial and error, our company slowly grew. People joined our ranks one at a time, and although I was a novice myself, I trained each of them, one by one. A high percentage worked part time—some had additional jobs while others were stay-at-home moms wanting to make extra money. A main attraction was the flexible work schedule we offered.

To the part-timers, a Pampered Chef career was not a top priority. So not unlike other direct-sales companies, our sales force had a constant turnover of people. Some left because they put little time into it and received little in return. Some worked only until they found full-time employment. Others moved on when their spouses were transferred out of town. Was it disappointing to lose someone, especially a Kitchen Consultant that I had high hopes for? You bet. But it happened again and again, and I learned to live with it. That's the nature of the business. I remember when Kim Bass broke it to me that her husband had taken a job in Wisconsin.

"You were our first Kitchen Consultant, Kim, and now you'll be our first to move from Chicago to Wisconsin," I said, trying to give it a positive spin.

"I don't think I can do it there," she said. "I'll be living in a rural area, and all of our people work in Chicago suburbs."

"Sure you can," I said, not really knowing for sure because it had never been done before.

"And now that my children are older, I feel I should spend more time with them."

I hated to see her go and I told her that the door was always open for her to rejoin the company. We kept in touch and remained good friends.

It is always disappointing to lose a Kitchen Consultant, especially as a small company. We were a close-knit group. I knew everybody, and I felt personally responsible for making sure each of them succeeded. When we were still small, I enclosed a handwritten note with every commission check, offering encouragement to those who needed it. I mailed out birthday cards and Christmas cards. I knew most of their children by name. When Consultants came to the office, their children would run into my office to give me hugs and kisses. I loved those visits; they made my day! We were a family business. Today, although the company is too big to know everybody and their children, the warmth we enjoyed in the 1980s has become deeply ingrained in our culture.

When it became apparent that the company would expand beyond a one-woman enterprise, I realized how important it was for me to communicate frequently and honestly with everyone in the organization. This was critical in making sure all of us were consistent in promoting our message. And it was critical to maintaining standards of ethical conduct.

Early on, when The Pampered Chef was a one-woman show, my personal standards of ethical conduct were the standards the business followed. The values I respected—integrity, determination, hard work, and respect for others—set the tone. Later, I had to communicate those values so everyone would know what was expected of him or her. I had to weave those values into the very fabric of the company.

Early on, this was fairly easy to do. After all, every Kitchen Consultant in the world still met in my living room for monthly sales meetings. We shared ideas and learned from each other as we developed the business. Each new Kitchen Consultant contributed her own creativity and energy to move The Pampered Chef.

I realized early on that direct selling requires the highest level of personal integrity. Kitchen Shows are unique because we conduct business in people's homes, surrounded by the host's invited guests. We call people by name and talk about our families. We describe the Pampered Chef opportunity and invite them to share it with us. This is an exceptionally personal level of selling. Personal trust is absolutely essential.

At first the only people who joined our company were women, many of whom had no experience in business. I thought of myself as a coach. Many of them looked to me as a role model, knowing I would make decisions that would affect their success with The Pampered Chef. Before long, I found myself acting as a leader, a role I hadn't sought, but one that evolved out of my feeling of responsibility to those who joined our company.

A NEW WAY OF SELLING

As you will recall, I had no prior direct-selling experience. I had no business experience at all! I didn't even consider our Kitchen Shows selling. The truth is I'm basically a shy person. I don't have the stereotypical sales personality, gregarious and outgoing. Fortunately, that's not what it takes to do well in this business.

Rather than persuasive selling skills, a Kitchen Consultant must be armed with information and product knowledge—this is what gives him or her self-confidence, and confidence *is* crucial. Certainly being an extrovert is not a liability, but an outgoing personality without know-how doesn't cut it. The fact is, our top performers don't sell—they teach. Like any good teacher, a Kitchen Consultant is a nurturer, and nurturing, I believe, comes naturally to women. Attending a Pampered Chef Kitchen Show is indeed a nurturing experience! Furthermore, we are teaching our customers to be more nurturing to *their* families.

So I created a sales presentation that I myself would enjoy watching. I did it without marketing data or surveys. Instead I offered a unique, interactive, multisensory experience: Kitchen Show guests see and touch our tools. They can smell the aroma of a simply wonderful recipe cooking, and savor its taste a few minutes later. This experience takes place in the comfort of home, surrounded by friends, and presented by a friendly, knowledgeable Kitchen Consultant. Initially my customer base was my friends and their friends. The last thing in the world I wanted to do was to use high-pressure tactics on them.

As a result, at a Pampered Chef Kitchen Show, we do not use high pressure. Our consultants are trained to provide information about our products, and they do it by demonstrating how to use them properly. Afterward, they rely on the quality of our products to sell them. Women come to learn and have fun with their friends. They kibitz, exchange recipes—and eat deliciously prepared food.

We don't teach traditional sales techniques to our sales field. They sell by their very enthusiasm and knowledge of our product. Over the years, I've had salespeople from other companies try various closing techniques on me; I'm familiar with what goes on out there.

For instance, I know that salespeople are trained to use the assumptive close.

"Do you want the large size or the super large size?"

"Do you want it in red or blue?"

"Do you want two or three units?"

"Do you want to pay by check or credit card?"

"We accept MasterCard and American Express. Which one do you want to charge it to?"

Each of the above questions offers an either-or choice; the salesperson assumes the prospect is buying, and uses that assumption to close the sale.

Another typical closing technique creates a sense of urgency. A salesperson might say, "Place an order today because we have limited inventory." The customer is being pressured to make a quick decision or he or she will lose out. I remember a car salesman who used this close when I was shopping for a car. "The new models due out next month will have a substantial increase in price," he told me. "This is the last car we have in this year's model."

A real estate agent once told Jay and me, "Three other couples are interested in this house."

"But it's been on the market for four months," Jay said.

"I know, but they just reduced the price. I advise you to make an offer right now; if you don't, it won't be available by the end of the day."

A friend of mine told me about a vacation time-sharing sales-man who made a limited offer by saying, "If you buy a unit to-day, there is a two-thousand-dollar discount."

"But we want to sleep on it," my friend said.

"Your night's sleep will be an expensive one. Because you'll have to pay two thousand more in the morning."

All of us have been exposed to high-pressure selling. Sales-people know that people tend to procrastinate when asked to make a buying decision. Salespeople know that if a prospect doesn't buy today, his or her enthusiasm will cool off, and the sale may be lost. At The Pampered Chef, we simply don't do it. Instead, we put the emphasis on product knowledge. Simply put, we show our products and they sell themselves. We're there to assist.

My philosophy has always been to focus on maximizing the sale versus closing it. I've always been low key, so much so, in fact, that I don't even ask for the order. We let the food, the tools, and their quality do the talking. Our products are reasonably priced, so there is no reason to pressure anyone to buy something she or he cannot afford. Since we offer our products in a variety of price ranges, people can easily find something that fits their pocketbook. It just so happens people tend to spend more when a product is demonstrated.

We do train our consultants to cross-sell, which has a dove-tailing effect. What do I mean by that? When a customer indi-cates she wants to buy a cookware product, a consultant might follow up by emphasizing that one of our nylon tools can be used with nonstick cookware to prevent damage to the cookware sur-face. Offering such suggestions increases the consultant's sales volume. Although cross-selling does augment the order, I don't consider it a form of high-pressure selling. The customer is free to decline the optional items.

Our Kitchen Consultants are also taught to be good listeners. They listen carefully when their customers ask questions during a show. Customers ask good questions and our Consultants pick up clues on which products are of interest. For instance, if a woman cooks for a large family instead of just one or two people, I know which pizza stone is appropriate for her. Does a customer do a lot of everyday cooking? Or is she more into holiday cooking? This information enables a consultant to demonstrate and recommend appropriate kitchen tools.

For the first five years in business, I paid little attention to what other companies did. As far as I was concerned, that didn't matter—what mattered was what we did. In 1986 the company joined the Direct Selling Association, a trade group, to learn what other companies do so we could tailor programs we felt would work for our company. It was a good move. I've met some very smart and highly professional members active in DSA, from whom I've learned a lot.

THE HEART AND SOUL OF OUR BUSINESS

My husband Jay is the ultimate entrepreneur. During our early years, he was always looking for opportunities and willing to take a risk if it could enhance our business.

One time a company approached us to serve as its distribution center because we had extra capacity in our building. It would have brought in additional revenue, and we had the skills to do it. It was tempting. It would have provided a stream of revenue that the company desperately needed. Just the same, I vetoed it, because I felt it would have taken our focus from our core business.

With my parents outside
our house on my
confirmation day,
April 1959.

With my sisters,
Barbara and Donna.

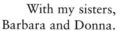

Eighth-grade graduation,
June 1959.

My father, Edward Kelley,
servicing a car at the gas
station he owned,
circa 1967.

Our class picture from my student teaching days, 1967—wearing the clothes that we made in class.

With Jay before our junior/senior prom—taken at the front porch of my house, June 1962.

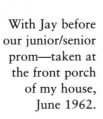

Jay and I on our wedding day, 1967.

Posing in my home kitchen for a photo that appeared in a local newspaper—among The Pampered Chef's first media coverage.

Jay's and my suburban Chicago home, the birthplace of The Pampered Chef.

Both of my daughters were involved in the business from an early age, helping out after school and on weekends. Here Kelley is stamping the Pampered Chef logo on bags in the basement.

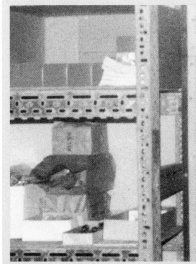

In the living room at home, rehearsing for my first Kitchen Show.

Consultants meeting around our dining room table during one of our
Saturday morning sales meetings.

Consultants at our first National Conference, held in Oak Park, Illinois, in September 1985.

My daughters, Julie and Kelley, get ready to deliver Kitchen Show orders with Mom and Dad.

Warren Buffett visits an Omaha-area Kitchen Show.

Our 2004 incentive trip to Kauai, Hawaii.

Warren Buffett shows off his culinary skills at a
Pampered Chef Kitchen Show.

Warren Buffett and I celebrate The Pampered Chef joining the Berkshire Hathaway family.

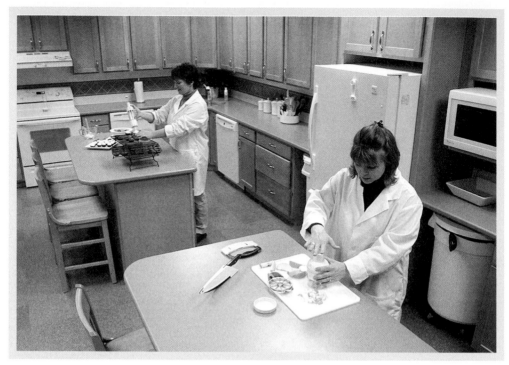

Two of our Test Kitchen professionals in one of our five Test Kitchens.

Our 780,000-square-foot Home Office and Distribution Center, which opened in 2002.

We were and are, first and foremost, a kitchen tools company; this is our singular purpose. Our focus is the Kitchen Show—the heart and soul of our company since the first day I loaded up my Volare and drove to my first show.

There have been enormous changes in the retail world since 1980—a time when home computers were still on the drawing board, Wal-Mart was a small regional entity, and the Internet was purely science fiction. Today, it seems every retailer tries to find the right balance of in-store, e-commerce, catalogs, discounting, and other sales channels. Over the years, many suggestions have been presented to us about how The Pampered Chef should distribute its products. The more we hear, the more convinced we are that the Kitchen Show will never be replaced. Along with the Kitchen Show, our sales organization is our company's most valuable asset.

NO PIE IN THE SKY

A handful of companies have promoted get-rich-quick schemes that have generated negative publicity. Known as pyramid organizations, their recruiting pitches make outrageous claims—that anyone can accumulate considerable wealth just by recruiting others into the business. On the order of a chain letter, the people at the top level make commissions from the fee people pay to join. These companies paint a vivid picture of the ease with which their associates become wealthy—practically overnight. "You too can be a millionaire," they tell potential recruits. Their top sales leaders address large audiences and boast of personal fortunes, which they attribute to the incredible opportunities available by joining their ranks. "Only two years ago, I was like you and had nothing," one of these charlatans crows. "Today, my wife and I live in a large mansion, we drive luxury foreign cars, wear expensive jewelry, and we travel first-class all over the world. If I can do it, so can any of you." They appeal to the poor and the gullible—individuals who are the most vulnerable.

Jay and I come from humble backgrounds, and being flashy is not our style. Even in the early days when I was just starting to recruit other people, I never talked about having a dream of building a large company. I never painted a picture of how successful I'd be. Nor did I assure anyone who joined in the beginning that he or she was getting in on the ground floor of a golden opportunity. Frankly, I had no idea that The Pampered Chef would become a large company. That wasn't even my goal.

My desires were modest. I simply wanted to teach people to perform better in the kitchen. I had no lofty goals of someday running a large organization. I didn't aspire to be wealthy. Later, I wanted to provide the opportunity to other women so that they, too, could enjoy flexible hours, working part time while continuing to be full-time mothers. I never told anyone they'd become rich in this business. I couldn't even imagine that I might someday become wealthy. I wanted to make only enough money for my children's college education. I didn't keep that a secret. I told women who joined our company about my ambition. "You could do the same thing for your children," I said. "Or make some extra money to save for a rainy day."

Money wasn't what motivated me to succeed, and I didn't want others working for The Pampered Chef who were driven by greed. I wanted women who had a desire to help other women—individuals who wanted to teach and to serve others.

Jay and I drove inexpensive cars, and we continued to live in our modest home for years after we were financially able to afford a nicer house. We took Julie and Kelley to vacation in the same area in Michigan that my family visited when I was young. And we waited until there was no more room in our home before we moved the business into our new building. We could have afforded to move sooner—and had we been out to make a big impression, we could have moved to fancier quarters. But we weren't trying to impress anyone. That's not who we are. We are middle America. We'd rather downplay the success we enjoy.

Get-rich-quick companies typically require new recruits to buy thousands of dollars of merchandise. Once aboard, they sign up other new recruits to also buy thousands of dollars of merchandise. While money keeps changing hands, little merchandise is sold to actual customers. Other companies promote "success rallies" conducted in large arenas with thousands of attendees. Motivational products such as books, videos, and audiocassettes are sold that "guarantee" riches to those who subscribe to their teachings. Although some of what is sold has merit, those most likely to profit from these products are their sellers.

In contrast, a new Kitchen Consultant purchases a starter kit; its cost is a modest $90 and it contains about $350 worth of products. The kit contains everything that is needed to conduct a successful Kitchen Show. Neither The Pampered Chef nor anyone in the sales field makes anything when a new person signs up. Commissions and overrides are made only when merchandise is purchased by customers. While it is possible for our top sales associates to earn exceptional incomes, we don't promote it as a main reason to join The Pampered Chef.

STRUCTURING THE SALES ORGANIZATION

All Pampered Chef Kitchen Consultants and Directors are independent contractors. They are self-employed, with no fixed hours. They work whenever and wherever they want. There are no sales territories. They receive commissions and override commissions based on productivity. There are no guarantees or draws against commissions. Like all independent businesspeople, they are paid according to their performance. Every field representative enters the business as a Kitchen Consultant. He or she starts out by doing Kitchen Shows, just as I did.

The commission schedule that Jay formulated for Kim Bass has been tweaked from time to time, but Kitchen Consultants receive a minimum of 20 percent on their own sales. To arrive at this percentage, Jay studied other companies, then factored in what we could actually afford to pay.

We pay overrides to people in our sales field who recruit, train, and build their own sales organization. The first rung on the sales ladder to success is the first promotion—to become a Future Director. Future Directors have recruited two people who become active Kitchen Consultants. (An active Consultant is one who sells $200 a month in commissionable sales over the course of two months.) When a Future Director has recruited five active Kitchen Consultants, he or she becomes a Director, and the people who work under her are members of her "cluster." The next level in our sales organization, an Advanced Director, has two first-line Directors. The next level, a Senior Director, has four first-line Directors. After that comes an Executive Director, with eight first-line Directors. The next level, a Senior Executive Director, has sixteen first-line Directors. And finally, a National Senior Executive Director (isn't that a mouthful) still has sixteen first-line Directors, but at least four must be Advanced Directors, at least two must be Senior Directors, and at least one is an Executive Director.

Consultants earn commissions based on personal sales, as well as overrides from other Consultants that they have recruited. At the National Senior Executive Directors' level, our salespeople can earn six-figure incomes. Like other business opportunities, what you get out of it depends on what you put into it. Unlike most other business opportunities, however, the individual has almost no capital at risk.

Every person at every level of the sales field is required to do Kitchen Shows, even National Senior Executive Directors. This is so they can keep in touch with the Kitchen Show experience and with what customers want.

In 1983, Myra Martin became our first Director. She was the first Kitchen Consultant to actively recruit people. Before Myra, there was virtually no recruiting effort outside of the Kitchen Show experience, formerly our sole source for new recruits. A former schoolteacher, Myra saw the big picture beyond earning commissions from her personal sales production. She viewed this as an opportunity to build her own sales organization and earn substantial income from overrides. Not only was she successful in building her own sales organization, she brought in other people who were also successful.

At the time, all our salespeople were part-timers, mostly moms looking for supplementary income. Eventually the business evolved; many of our Kitchen Consultants see The Pampered Chef as an opportunity to make a full-time income—more money than they'd make at a full-time job elsewhere.

In 1986, Nancy Jo Ryan, a former accountant and stay-at-home mother of two little children, joined The Pampered Chef, intending to make extra money for the holiday season. Nancy Jo was an excellent salesperson, and as it turned out, she was also an outstanding recruiter and trainer. Convinced she had a mission to share this opportunity with other women, she recruited thirty-five people during her first year with us. Nancy Jo raised the bar for the rest of the organization, helping to develop other people within her own organization. One of the legends of our company, Nancy Jo is today a National Senior Executive Director and heads one of The Pampered Chef's largest sales groups.

MONTHLY MEETINGS

Even after we moved our operations to 340 Lathrop Avenue in 1985, I continued to conduct our monthly sales meetings at our home. First, we needed a kitchen, but even more important, I preferred a home atmosphere similar to that at a Kitchen Show. As the company grew, Kitchen Consultants from the Greater Chicago area attended; soon, some came in from northwestern Indiana and northern Illinois, all within driving distance. I chose Saturday mornings because it was not a particularly good time for Kitchen Shows, and Consultants who wanted to attend could easily find available babysitters for their children.

Most direct-sales organizations conduct weekly sales meetings, but I knew from personal experience that weekly meetings wouldn't have worked on my schedule, and that it was likely that other women felt the same way.

Every monthly meeting followed the same format: lots of information shared and lots of good food. Yes, it was partly social, but I made sure we covered enough business to make it worthwhile. Everyone seemed to enjoy the meetings, but at the same time, I knew they took valuable weekend time away from our Consultants' families, so I wanted to give them their money's worth. Certainly the meetings were good for morale, because to a Kitchen Consultant working out of her home, mixing with peers is reassuring and invigorating. And when a meeting was over, they left knowing that they learned something useful that could be applied to their work.

We didn't conduct the rah-rah-rah pep talk meetings that are routine with some direct-selling companies. Nor did we establish sales goals for our people. Like our Kitchen Shows, our meetings were low key. Furthermore, no pressure was put on anyone to meet sales quotas. We had a mission—to bring people together at mealtime. This was the focal point of our monthly meetings. And for those who wanted more from the business, it was there for them to take.

I was pleased to discover a genuine willingness to share ideas at these meetings. There was lots of talk about the Consultants' success, as well as their trials and tribulations of the past thirty days, and offers of suggestions on how to overcome them. No one dwelled on the negative. If someone was having a problem, we focused on solving it and moving forward. And the consultants felt confident that what they learned from their peers had been field-tested and proven.

Later, one Consultant, Sue Rusch, moved from Chicago to Minneapolis, and continued to build her business there. Sue still had family in Chicago, so for her first six months in Minneapolis, she returned to attend our monthly meetings. After she recruited some people in her new hometown, she and I decided it was time for her to conduct her own meetings the same Saturday of the month I did mine. A few days beforehand, we would talk on the phone and plan the agenda for the meeting, then we'd run the same meeting in Chicago and in Minneapolis.

In due course, our small house could no longer accommodate all of our Consultants. Then too, new recruits were spread out; logistically, it wasn't feasible for them to drive long distances to attend my Saturday morning meetings. At this point, other Directors started conducting sales meetings for their own clusters; sometimes two would team up and do it together. One Director on the South Side of Chicago conducted a monthly meeting on a weekday evening, and she teamed up with another Director who did hers on Saturday morning. Their Consultants could choose the meeting that fit their schedules.

OUR FIRST NATIONAL CONFERENCE

We held our first Pampered Chef National Conference on September 14, 1985. A one-day event, it took place at the Carleton Hotel in Oak Park, adjacent to River Forest and about ten miles from downtown Chicago. We had picked the Carleton because it had formerly been a residence hotel, and each suite was equipped with a small kitchen with a small oven and refrigerator. Workshops were conducted throughout the entire day, for which we needed kitchen facilities. The biggest attraction of the day was witnessing Kitchen Show demonstrations by our top people. That first conference we had a 100 percent turnout—all thirty-two of our Consultants attended.

Our first conference theme was "The Sky's the Limit with The Pampered Chef." With his previous experience at setting up sales meetings for Lien Chemical, Jay helped plan it. The highlight of the day was the awards banquet, where we recognized our top performers. Silver bowls were awarded in three categories: top Director, top recruiters, and top seller. Their names were engraved on a roster plaque that is permanently displayed at our company office. The event was a big success, and it set the tone for our future annual conferences.

A small company, we wanted everyone to feel like a member of our family, and to help create this warm atmosphere, we made sure they got to know our family. My mother and Jay's parents were regular guests of honor. Our daughters Julie and Kelley also got into the act. One year at the Sheraton Hotel in Arlington Heights we announced a contest to take our top producers to Disney World. By this time Kelley was in junior high. We had her dress up in a Minnie Mouse costume to greet our Consultants.

Working on a low budget, our early conferences were far less extravagant than today's, which take place annually at Mc-Cormick Place Convention Center in Chicago during the month of July. Today, we can't accommodate everyone at a single conference: we have three consecutive conferences, each with an attendance of about four thousand. These events are professionally produced, with every detail planned in advance. Professional speakers are brought in and workshops are conducted with smaller groups throughout the three days. Between presentations, professional dancers and singers liven things up.

As at our first conference, we continue to recognize our star performers. Each year every individual who has been promoted to a higher level is recognized on stage in the presence of thousands of peers. I personally congratulate each of them on stage, with a hug and hearty handshake. And I'm pleased to say I've done a lot of hugging and handshaking over the years! I know how hard they worked to achieve their goals. From what I've been told by our sales organization, our tradition of marching our star performers on stage is a strong motivator to those in the audience who hope to be recognized themselves at future conferences. There is also an exclusive special reception held at the national conference in recognition of top performers.

Early on, with limited funds, Jay and I brought furniture from our home to our Pampered Chef conferences to use as props. One time our staff filled hundreds of balloons with helium—but evidently not enough helium. As I stood at the podium speaking, the balloons began to descend. As I continued my speech, the balloons continued their slow but steady fall. Everyone was distracted. To my good fortune, just as the balloons were inches from my head, I finished. As they say in the theater, the show must go on.

PRAISING PEOPLE TO SUCCESS

Beginning with my first Kitchen Show, I discovered how much I enjoyed the kudos I received from guests. It was music to my ears to hear someone say:

"I've got to get this tool."

"I didn't know such a thing existed. And now that I have it, I use it all the time."

"I tried this recipe and now my husband and children beg me to make it all the time."

To my surprise, I realized that I thrived on being able to help people, and the positive reinforcement was invigorating. To quote Mark Twain, "I could live two months on a good compliment."

Sure, I had my share of disappointments along the way, but it's amazing how quickly I forgot them when I received praise at a Kitchen Show. And what made it so wonderful was that it happened all the time. The human spirit thrives on positive reinforcement—we all need to be praised for our achievements. As other people joined our ranks, I became aware that they, too, thrived on the praise they received at Kitchen Shows. Consequently, we constantly praise and recognize our people for their performances. I like to say we praise people to success.

At our company gatherings, ranging from our national sales conferences to leadership meetings conducted across the country, our top achievers wear ribbons with colors that designate their rank within our organization. For newcomers, we have a booklet that lists what the colors of the ribbons mean. For example, a Director wears a red ribbon. The color orange means the wearer is on the Product Advisory Committee, and so on. As you can imagine, some women are decorated with many ribbons, each representing a different achievement. Likewise, we have corporate jewelry that is awarded in recognition for top performances. There is a bar pin that has a gold whisk, to which diamonds are added based on annual performance. For our very top achievers, rings and other jewelry are awarded. Our people wear their jewelry to our conferences, and like decorated military officers are recognized by their medals and ribbons.

One of the highest honors we bestow on our people is the Legacy Award, a special recognition that has been presented only six times in our history. The recipient is an individual who has done something extraordinary over a period of time that has had a positive impact on the company as a whole. It's akin to the Lifetime Achievement Award presented at the motion picture industry's Academy Awards. The last person to receive the Legacy Award was Barbara Duke for her pioneering work in California in the early 1990s. I'll tell you more about Barbara in Chapter 8.

I had the privilege of presenting this honor to Barbara at our 2000 National Conference before an audience of four thousand Pampered Chef people.

As a way to help motivate our sales force, we held an annual sales contest, beginning in 1986. By the early and mid-1980s, we were experimenting with different incentives to award to our people. After joining the Direct Selling Association in 1986, I remember coming home from a meeting excited about what I learned about travel incentives that other companies were using.

"These other companies are getting tremendous results by taking their top producers on fantastic trips," I told Jay. "From what I can see, this really turns salespeople on."

"Why so?"

"You know, Jay, look at us. We've never been able to take dream vacations to the Caribbean, Hawaii, and Europe. And how our mouths water when our friends take one of those trips."

"Where would you take them?" Jay asked.

"Cancun, Mexico, is a popular destination," I suggested. "That would make a nice first trip."

"I know what this is all about," Jay teased. "You just want to go someplace warm and sunny."

Jay and I determined how much sales production would qualify a Kitchen Consultant for a trip for two, and then I announced the contest and its rules. "The winners will receive an all-expenses-paid trip to Cancun for two this coming January 1987. The sales numbers necessary to win are achievable for everybody, and we hope that all of you and your spouses will be joining my husband and me in Cancun."

Our contests are set up so everyone can win. This way, nobody competes against other Pampered Chef people; the more that achieve enough sales to win a trip, the merrier.

LaVerne Soltys and Cindy Marazas qualified for the Cancun trip. Jay couldn't go because his father had a stroke shortly before we were scheduled to leave. So I invited my good friend Harriet Nelson, as a way of paying her back for the support she gave me in the summer of 1980 when The Pampered Chef was still in its conceptual stage. LaVerne's and Cindy's husbands came as well, and the six of us had a ball. The following year, our second incentive trip took the company's achievers to Jamaica, and this time, Jay came along. He hasn't missed an incentive trip since.

Travel incentives work particularly well with young couples, because they are often reluctant to treat themselves to a vacation when there are many other family needs to consider. A getaway vacation for a married couple with children can seem frivolous compared to buying back-to-school clothes or painting the house. This is what makes a well-earned vacation so special. The fact that they've earned it and we're picking up the tab gives them permission to indulge themselves.

Knowing that there will be some people who qualify for vacations but cannot come because of a conflict, a new baby, medical emergencies, and so forth, we give them other options.

On a recent trip to San Diego, we had a party of 1,600 Pampered Chef Consultants and their families. One of them said to me: "This is our family vacation this year, but we could never have stayed in a hotel of this caliber!" Another said, "This is my first trip to California." And still another said, "I've never been on an airplane before."

Jay and I love to see the faces of their children as they get off the airplane in Orlando and board the bus to Disney World. We're right there with them on the buses to the hotel; some of those children have been talking about their Disney World trip for a year. And these kids deserve it—they helped Mom with her business, so they feel rewarded too.

Today's travel incentives make it possible for anyone who meets the goal to qualify. In fact, the percentages of our people who earn travel rewards are proportionately higher than those of most other direct-sales companies. (In 2003 a Consultant with sales of $18,500 earned $3,700 in commissions, plus a certificate for a two-night stay at any of 120 hotels across the country. For those with sales in excess of $70,000, we awarded them a four-day trip for two to Hawaii.) Since that first trip to Cancun, we have taken our Consultants to Paris, Rome, and Hawaii. Our top Directors have been invited on executive trips to such faraway places as Hong Kong and Australia.

We try to mix up our destinations; some are family-oriented and others are designed to let couples escape by themselves for a romantic getaway.

One of the biggest benefits that we at The Pampered Chef receive from these trips is the spouses' reactions. A husband will see other men who are supportive of their wives—they have jobs, same-age kids, and lifestyles like his. "These are good people," he realizes, "and they're really into their wives' career. I'm going to be more supportive to my wife, as well."

I love it when a husband says to me, "What I'm enjoying most about this experience, Doris, is seeing my wife bask in the glory of her accomplishment."

EARLY RECRUITING EFFORTS

In direct selling, recruiting salespeople is crucial. It didn't take me long to find out that our best source for new recruits was our

Kitchen Show guests themselves. I could talk all day about a Kitchen Show, but there is nothing like experiencing it. Seeing is believing. The Kitchen Show's entertaining atmosphere makes it fun, and our Consultants are constantly teaching useful kitchen techniques. They teach more than they sell.

Our flexible hours are also a major attraction to people considering a Pampered Chef career. It was obvious to guests at my early Kitchen Shows that my hours were flexible. Other women wanted the same opportunity. I always placed the needs of my family before my work; in doing so, I was living proof that they could do it too.

In the beginning people asked, "Doris, how do you expect to build a business by working only part time? Doesn't a start-up business require sixty to eighty hours a week to succeed?"

As things turned out, had I worked at The Pampered Chef on a full-time basis, it probably would have backfired. Other women, seeing me put in long hours, would think they'd also have to do the same as a Kitchen Consultant. But when they saw I worked part time and still functioned as a full-time mother for Julie and Kelley, they liked it. I was doing something they could emulate.

Once I realized I could recruit and train other women, I envisioned a sales organization that would someday sell our products throughout the Midwest. I didn't give serious thought to having Kitchen Consultants in other areas of the country, although it did occur to me that there might be a few Consultants who moved to neighboring states, especially Indiana. East Chicago, Indiana, is less than thirty minutes from the Loop in downtown Chicago. But those who moved too far away to attend our monthly meetings were the first to fall by the wayside. While I understood in theory that a strong Director could build her own cluster away from our headquarters, it was easier said than done. No one had yet done it, and we didn't know it was possible. Some felt it was unrealistic to think we would ever expand beyond the local area. Meanwhile, there was so much work to do in Chicago that there wasn't much point in thinking about faraway markets.

By 1988, we had Consultants in downstate Illinois, as well as in Indiana, Michigan, Wisconsin, and also Minnesota. To my pleasant surprise, we discovered that a strong Director working closely with our home office by long-distance phone could successfully develop her own cluster of Kitchen Consultants. Distance, we discovered, was no deterrent. The expansion of our sales organization into other markets, however, could not rest solely on the few Consultants and Directors who moved out of state. Eventually, I realized I needed to travel to open up new areas.

One of my first recruiting trips centered on Indianapolis, a three-and-a-half-hour drive from Chicago. I decided to attend the annual meeting of the American Home Economics Association scheduled there. While I was in town, I placed an ad in the newspaper to conduct interviews. I was anxious to see what results I could get from out-of-town newspaper ads; from Indianapolis, I extended my trip west to St. Louis. Chicago, Indianapolis, and St. Louis form an equilateral triangle, each within an easy drive from the others. I figured if I could get some Kitchen Consultants in these cities, I could return to support them. Along the way, I planned stops in Terre Haute, Indiana, as well as O'Fallon, Effingham, and Belleville, small towns in Illinois.

I wasn't sure what would result from this whirlwind recruiting trip. As it turned out, I was in for a real learning experience. At the American Home Economics Association's meeting, one home economist executive from a national food company said to me, "So you sell things that people can buy anywhere."

"Yes," I answered, "but we provide services that they don't receive elsewhere."

"Do professional home economists sell these products for you?" she asked.

"We have some people that are home economists, but far more of our people come from all different backgrounds."

She looked at me and said, "I don't know why anyone would buy those things from you. People aren't cooking anymore. People can't even read anymore. We put the most simple language on packaging because our research tells us that people today are illiterate."

"I don't find that's true of my customers," I said. "My customers are eager for information. They are excited about the things they can learn. And they read very well."

She gave me a cold stare and walked away.

I thought to myself, here's the department head of a Fortune 500 company who has a poor opinion of her customers. Her disdain upset me. I had personal contact with our customers, and they are smart, informed consumers. She's so far removed from hers that she can't possibly know what I know. I refused to allow this woman to deflate my confidence. Instead, I decided to prove her wrong.

Being on the road was difficult. First, like most mothers with young children, I felt guilty being away from them for several days on a business trip. Second, there were days when I set up five to ten interviews, and frequently half the people didn't show up, and the other half had no interest in our company. I'd call Jay at night to report my day's progress, and though I tried to maintain my good spirits, he could tell from my voice when I had a challenging day. "Don't let it get you down," he'd tell me. "Everyone has his share of bad days in business."

"You're right, honey," I'd say, my spirits lifted. "I miss you, and tell the girls that I love them."

A young woman from Terre Haute had called me in Chicago in response to a newspaper ad, and I promised to contact her while I was in Indianapolis.

"Let's see, Terre Haute is about eighty miles southwest of Indianapolis," I said to her while studying a map. "I'll swing by Terre Haute on my way to St. Louis. Where's a good place for us to meet for a cup of coffee when I get there?"

"Would you mind coming to my house?" she asked. "I don't have a car available to drive to see you."

Although I didn't feel comfortable about it, I consented. When I pulled up in front of her rickety house, I felt uneasy. It was located in a very poor area; looking through the wide-open front door I could see bare mattresses on the living room floor. I rechecked the address to make sure I was at the right place. There were three small children on the front porch. It was obvious they were expecting me because they yelled, "Mommy, Mommy, someone is here! Someone is here!"

A young, disheveled woman came out the door wearing a tattered cotton dress. She had missing teeth and looked like she might have been a battered wife. She called me by name and waved to me to get out of the car. There was no porch furniture, but she invited me to sit with her on the front steps. I was dressed professionally; I felt ill at ease because she kept apologizing for her appearance. "It doesn't matter," I tried to reassure her. It was difficult to talk because her children constantly needed her attention. Still, I did my best to give her a complete rundown on The Pampered Chef. I am sure she answered the ad because she desperately needed a way to earn some money. If ever there was a poor candidate for The Pampered Chef, however, she was it.

As we talked, I thought of ways I might be able to help her. I was determined to treat her just as I would the most promising interviewee.

I ended my conversation by leaving her with company literature, saying, "Please call me if you wish to pursue this further."

"Oh, yes, I'm going to think about it," she answered. "Thank you so much for coming!"

After I left her house, I never heard from this woman again.

My eyes welled up with tears as I got back on the highway to St. Louis. This woman was such a contrast to the professional women I met in Indianapolis. So much for my first interview! Yet I felt so bad for this woman and her children. Seeing them made me think about my two children I had left at home during this business trip. Where are my priorities? I asked myself. Why am I so far away from them? Upon arriving in St. Louis, I checked into a hotel room where I had scheduled several interviews with local women, again from ads I had placed in the local newspapers. Fortunately, these interviews went smoothly and resulted in signing up a few new Kitchen Consultants. One of these new recruits was Irene Heisler, who today is a Director.

Always looking for ways to recruit in other markets outside Chicago, I talked to a friend who was chairman of the University of Illinois Band Boosters Mothers' Club. She asked if I could do Pampered Chef fund-raisers across the state of Illinois. I agreed. "I will give Kitchen Shows in cities and towns at the homes of the university's alumni. And while our practice is to give a percentage of the sales to a host, instead the money will go to your organization."

She consented. Whenever a Kitchen Show was set up to raise money for the school's Band Boosters Mothers' Club, I would place a recruiting ad in the local newspaper in advance. As I interviewed women, I'd say to any interested candidates, "I'm having a Kitchen Show in town; you should come with me to see firsthand what this is all about." This worked liked a charm, and before long we were off to the races. Women across central Illinois and in bordering states were becoming Kitchen Consultants.

RECRUITING RANDY WEISS

Perhaps the highlight of that three-state recruiting trip was meeting Randy Weiss in St. Louis in early July. Randy was scheduled to meet me at my hotel but made a last-minute call to cancel the appointment.

"I'm so sorry," she apologized, "but with the long weekend coming up, I just can't make it in to see you. Can we do it some other time?"

There was something about Randy's personality on the telephone that made me instantly like her. I had a feeling she had great potential for the business. Evidently I must have erased that Terre Haute woman from my mind, because I found myself saying to Randy, "If you can't come to me, I'll come to you."

"We just had a big family party," she said. "My house is a mess."

"That's okay," I said. "I'll come tomorrow morning." Even as I said the words, I surprised myself. It's not like me to be so persistent and not to take no for an answer.

"Okay, if you want to come," she said, "come."

She gave me directions, and I went to see her the following morning. This was the last interview of my recruiting trip—later that afternoon, Jay and the girls were flying to St. Louis and we would spend the Fourth of July weekend sightseeing. Randy welcomed me to her house and we talked for about an hour. Both she and her husband seemed very interested.

"I want you to see a Kitchen Show," I told them, "so here's what we'll do. If you'll host one at your home, I'll come back to conduct it. Once you see it, you can decide if this is for you."

Randy consented, and I headed to the airport to pick up my family. I was on cloud nine.

It wasn't until late September when I actually did a show at

Randy's house. In the interim, I made two more trips to St. Louis to meet with Irene and the other people I had recruited in the St. Louis area, and each time, I made a special effort to visit Randy. She was still undecided on our business. Her tentative nature, which had allowed me to get in the door, was now keeping me at bay. She simply wasn't going to make a quick decision on this. Finally I did the Kitchen Show at Randy's house. I thought it was really going well, but in the middle of the show, I overheard her mother saying to the person next to her, "I don't know why Randy is fooling around with this. She's a good nurse, and she has her training. Why would she do something like this?"

When I heard that, my heart sank. I thought Randy had already made the decision to join the company, but from what her mother had said, her family was trying to talk her out of it.

Nonetheless, after the show, Randy said to me, "I'm ready. I want to do this." I was elated.

I made several more trips to St. Louis to visit Irene and our other people, always spending time with Randy. Before long, she started recruiting people, and her career really took off. Today, Randy is one of an elite handful of National Senior Executive Directors. She has been a real force in our business.

NEVER PREJUDGE

Over the years, I learned I should never prejudge anyone. Experience has proven that prospective Kitchen Consultants are not easily predictable. Just when I would think that someone was going to be dynamite, she would disappoint me, and conversely, others that I thought looked mediocre became superstars.

But one thing I was sure of: the best people are recruited from our Kitchen Shows. These people see it, and they *get* it. They don't have to be talked into it. They say to themselves, "I know I can do this," and they're right. Those who are tentative and have to be talked into it generally don't make it. Randy Weiss was an exception. I believed she had star potential for the business from the day I met her

On the same trip to St. Louis when I met Randy, I interviewed a woman who worked in an upscale kitchen retail store. I thought she would be fabulous for our business. She was somebody who knew and appreciated high-quality kitchen tools. But it turned out her background in retailing worked against her. She was used to having the store's merchandise presented in perfect condition, just as it is when it's sitting on the shelf. She wanted our products to look sparkling brand-new, just out of the box—that was her mind-set. Consequently, she felt uncomfortable using our products at Kitchen Shows. She couldn't adjust to our hands-on presentations where we actually use products versus simply displaying them. Hence her Pampered Chef career was short-lived.

Today I tell our people: "You can never judge somebody walking in the door. There have been too many times when I've predicted that a person filled with self-confidence will be a top seller with two hundred and fifty people under her. And how many times have I been wrong. Then there's the quiet woman who comes in—the wallflower you suspect doesn't have a clue what this business is about—and ten years later, she's a top performer!"

BEHIND EVERY SUCCESSFUL WOMAN . . .

Occasionally at a Pampered Chef gathering Jay will walk around with a name tag, and under his name is the title "First Spouse."

Jay says it serves as an icebreaker to start conversations with a Kitchen Consultant's spouse. (Not that he needs one; my husband is not the bashful type.)

"The attitude of the spouse," he says, "is what makes or breaks the Consultant. If he is not supportive, the odds are slim that she will succeed. When I meet husbands, one of the first questions I'll ask is, 'What was your first reaction when your wife told you she was going to spend ninety dollars to buy these kitchen tools?'

"Some spouses respond by saying, 'This will be wonderful for you.' Others jump in with all kinds of objections, without having a clue about this business."

Jay frequently conducts Spouse workshops at various company functions. While the Kitchen Consultants are attending workshops, Jay monitors a panel with three or four husbands who talk to a group of spouses. He'll ask husbands such questions as: "How do you view the perks of being a Pampered Chef spouse?" "What are your thoughts on the incentive travel?" "What has this business meant to your family?" "Let's talk about the changes that have occurred as a result of your wife running a business out of your house."

He doesn't pull any punches when he talks to the spouses. "How will you feel when you go to your job every day that you can't stand, but she is loving her work? There may come a time for some of you when your wife's income takes off. While you're receiving only three or four percent increases in your salary every year, her earnings double year after year. This is something you must be prepared to face. Because it's quite possible she'll be making more income than you. How will you react to that? Will your male ego get in the way? Will you unconsciously start to undermine her Pampered Chef business? Or are you going to encourage and support her, and together enjoy the fruits of her enterprise? Is your wife a former wallflower? How will you react when she's speaking with confidence to large groups and growing her business? How do you deal with that change in your life?"

The two of us have discussed this subject endlessly and we have concluded that there are three types of spouses. The first is the most effective because this person is realistic and at the same time positive about the business. The second type peacefully coexists with his or her mate's business. He or she doesn't go out of the way to be supportive but is there. The third type is the worst, because this person constantly seeks ways to sabotage his spouse. He has low self-esteem and acts out of fear. His fear is that as his spouse grows, he will feel less important. It is my strong belief that ultimately a Kitchen Consultant with an antagonistic spouse should seriously consider whether she should continue in our business.

Family harmony is essential for a person working out of her home. When a Kitchen Consultant encounters antagonism from her husband, I often recommend considering another career. Her marriage is more important than this business; unless she is able to resolve issues on the home front, she should consider another career. Of course, there are always compromises. Couples should discuss issues and objections that come up; generally, they can work around them. For example, telephone calls at dinnertime can be banished, business conversations over dinner can be reduced, work schedules can be adjusted, and so on. If a Kitchen Consultant is unable to work out the issues, however, and if the antagonism and confrontation continue at home, then this business isn't for her.

FEEDBACK FROM THE FIELD

I once heard a Fortune 500 company CEO say that if he listens carefully to the people at different levels of his organization, it eliminates the need to hire outside consultants. "All of the solutions to any problem can be found within our own organization," he insisted. "By looking deep into our company and listening to our people at their job sites—workers who spend eight hours a day at their jobs—I am privy to information I need to know to fix things. These people know their jobs better than any outside consultant. The secret is to be a good listener. Listen, and they will tell you how to fix a problem. What's more, they're delighted to tell you. All you have to do is hear them out."

I learned this firsthand by being in the field with my salespeople for many years. I personally saw many ideas out there, waiting to be picked—I just had to be quiet and listen. Today, with 70,000-plus Kitchen Consultants meeting with an estimated twelve million customers a year, we have an enormous reservoir from which to draw information to find out what our customers are thinking. As a result, we don't have to wait for a customer to take the time to let us know what she thinks. We're often in front of an audience, our sales organization, that is very vocal and very tuned in. They willingly share their thoughts with us. Keep in mind that they are independent—The Pampered Chef is not their boss. There is no restraint on what they say to us. When there is a problem, we quickly hear about it. Our management team is never kept in the dark.

Unlike some companies that have to conduct surveys to find out what their customers are thinking, our sales force is as close as you can get to customers—in their homes! This is a very close connection. They are our source of dependable information about our customers. And in fact, they mirror our customer, because they started out as customers themselves. By tapping into this valuable source of information, we have been able to respond quickly. Unlike many large companies, we don't need months of consumer research to gather their opinions.

As a result, we work especially hard to keep an open line of communication with our sales organization—something I think is important in every company. While it's not possible to respond to the opinions of all 70,000 Kitchen Consultants, we have many standing committees that meet on a regular basis. These committees consist of a cross section of our sales organization ranging from our most experienced National Senior Executive Directors to Kitchen Consultants. If our committees had only senior people, we might get a one-sided message. We also benefit from the fact that every Director and Executive Director and so on has risen through the ranks. And even the most senior Directors continue to host a minimum of one Kitchen Show a month themselves, so they know firsthand what is going on in the field. It's a practice I would recommend other businesses consider emulating.

I am constantly attending committee meetings with people in our sales organization. We have committees for long-term planning, product development, recipe development, and so on. At these meetings I always take notes and ask questions. "What do you need to make your business more successful?" I ask.

Well before we launch a new product, we run it by our people in the field. "Here's something we're considering. Do you think it will fly?" The consensus we gather enables us to avoid products that either don't sell or have other problems down the road. While there is no guarantee of success with any new product, our feedback from the field certainly increases our odds.

6
GROWING PAINS

In the mid-1980s, Jay accompanied me on a two-day recruiting trip to Fort Wayne, Indiana, a three-hour drive from Chicago. As we talked about how the company was growing, Jay said to me, "We should really have a written mission statement."

The next afternoon on the way back home, Jay said to me, "While you were in the room conducting interviews, I read a mission statement on the wall in the hotel lobby. I think that it pretty much matches our philosophy."

"What did it say?" I asked.

Jay pulled out some scratch paper and a pencil, and wrote the lines as he remembered them. We tweaked the one Jay saw on the hotel on the way home until we came up with an original statement of our own. At the time, company mission statements were just starting to get attention.

The mission statement we developed that day continues to guide us.

The Pampered Chef is committed to providing opportunities for individuals to develop their God-given talents and skills to their fullest potential for the benefit of themselves, their families, our customers, and the company. We are dedicated to enhancing the quality of family life by providing quality kitchen products, supported by service and information for our Consultants and customers.

At the end of his first month working full time for The Pampered Chef, Jay was handed a stack of seventy-five manila folders containing copies of each Consultant's sales for the month. Four of us had similar stacks of manila envelopes to go through. This was how we calculated our sales commissions back then. Each of us reviewed and calculated the total sales of every Consultant in our stack. Commission checks were always mailed the first day of the month. Because our calculations were done manually, they were prone to error. We worked on a tight deadline; due to time constraints, we rarely had the time to double-check the numbers.

After several months of this tedious manual process, Jay contacted several computer services companies for bids on a program to provide computer tear-out sheets for each Consultant, and commission checks corresponding with those statements. This rather mundane commissioning system marked the beginning of the company's information services. It was yet another sign of our continued growth.

To celebrate of our tenth anniversary in 1990, we made a prediction at our annual sales conference: "The Pampered Chef will someday have as many as six hundred Consultants in all fifty states." At the time we were operating in roughly forty states. The response to this bold forecast prompted a standing ovation.

Little did we know how quickly our business would grow. Today, whenever we play a videotape of this prediction, it is accompanied by roars of laughter. We've exceeded our prediction by over one hundred times.

Filled with confidence at the start of our second decade in business, we had no idea what the 1990s held in store. In March 1990, we added another facility to our building at 344 Lathrop Avenue. A new, larger facility at 7771 Van Buren in Forest Park doubled our warehouse and office space to ten thousand square feet, which we thought would be ample space for some time to come.

By the end of 1990, our annual sales had jumped to $10 million, up from $1 million in 1987. Clearly, our marketing concept and business model worked. We were no longer a tiny operation. As a result of our recruiting efforts and sales activity, we were growing by leaps and bounds. The company had mushroomed far beyond our initial expectations. Still, in many respects we operated much as we did in 1980, just on a much larger scale. Our game plan hadn't changed. It remained the same: go out there and educate. Every week we saw growth from all directions. We were recruiting Consultants, booking more shows, and sales were skyrocketing. I focused on the marketing side of the business; Jay worked to develop systems to accommodate our growth, always trying to stay ahead of the curve.

The previous year, our first national sales manager had calculated that the company would plateau at $19 million. Having worked with several direct-sales companies, he confidently told Jay, "I know this business. So enjoy this current growth spurt now, because down the road, it's going to fizzle." Shortly after his prediction, he quit to join another company, which, as it turns out, went belly up.

A VALUABLE LESSON

Shortly after we moved to our first building, I hired Joan Tomasello to be our office manager. She came highly recommended by Jay, who had worked with her at Lien Chemical for ten years. Joan knew Jay's management style and she quickly adapted to our company. Before long she was indispensable. I could leave the office for business travel for days at a time, knowing everything was in good hands. She was a real take-charge person, just the kind of office manager I needed.

In my absence, the Kitchen Consultants who called in talked to Joan. They called to check on the status of a pending order, or to request sales materials. Joan fielded their calls like a pro, and her winning personality made her a favorite with our field organization. Now remember, our Kitchen Consultants are independent contractors; they are not employees. In effect, our sales organization consists of an army of self-employed businesspeople, representing a diverse group. Their differences run the gamut in terms of age, education, job experience, and so on. Consequently, it is a real challenge to keep them motivated, excited, and dedicated. Being independent, they can be quite vocal in expressing their opinions. It is no walk in the park to be on the receiving end of a telephone call from a displeased Consultant. Nonetheless, Joan worked well with our Kitchen Consultants; they liked and respected her.

But Joan has never been accused of being a carbon copy of me. She is definitely her own person; she is decisive and never one to pull her punches. She "tells it like it is." Back then I tended to be more indecisive. After listening, I tended to say, "Well, now what do *you* think?"

One day while I was away on a business trip, a Kitchen Consultant called Joan, pleading, "I couldn't get my order in on time, but I really need it to be included in this past month's business. I really need the money."

"I'm sorry it wasn't on time," Joan responded. "And you know the rules; that's the way it is."

A day later, the Consultant came into my office holding a baby and holding the hand of another small child. Without mentioning her conversation with Joan, she told me, "My children were sick, Doris, and I couldn't get my order mailed in time. Please help me. I need the money."

I looked at her with her two small children and said, "Well, all right, this time. We'll make an exception." As she left, I walked over to Joan and said, "We're going to count her order for last month."

Joan just looked at me with a poker face. "Oh, we are? Okay." She didn't say another word. I knew she wasn't happy about it, but she did as I asked. She waited until the end of the day before coming to my office, just as I was heading out the door.

"Do you have a minute?" she asked.

I could sense she was upset about something. "Sure, sit down," I said, guiding us toward a couple of chairs.

"You know, Doris, I think you probably don't need me anymore," she said.

"What? What do you mean?"

"Well, if I'm going to uphold the rules, and you come back and bend the rules, then pretty soon nobody is going to believe anything I say."

I saw her point immediately. Joan was my right hand. I was focused on the sales, marketing, and product side of the business. She had taken over the operations and the managing of our internal people. I couldn't function without her. It was true she never went out to do Kitchen Shows, because she didn't have that piece of the business. But she owned the operations side. She worked closely with Jay. When I considered all the things that she did on a daily basis, I shuddered at the thought of managing them myself.

"Okay, Joan, I get it! I apologize. I'll do my best to make sure it doesn't happen again."

Joan's threat to leave was probably for effect; I knew she liked it here. Just the same, I learned a most valuable lesson. For the first time I realized that when I was out and handling the things I handled, others were managing and making the decisions in their areas. And I had to recognize that they were better able than I to make those decisions. Of course, this didn't mean I wouldn't be a last court of appeal, because on rare occasions a rule should be revisited. Nonetheless, it was at this moment that I realized this business had to be run by the rules. If not, every single thing would have to go before me, which would curtail the company's ability to grow and to attract strong people capable of thinking on their own. Joan was so right. If I was going to build a successful company, I had to give others authority and responsibility.

After discussing my encounter with Joan, Jay and I decided that the company was in dire need of a policies and procedures manual. We realized our chances of future success were dependent upon having structure. And once in place, it must be respected.

"That's not to say you never put on a room addition," Jay emphasized. "But we can't decide things on a case-by-case basis." I agreed.

We've followed this same philosophy over the years, and it's withstood the test of time. When someone says, "I don't think this is fair," we review rules to determine whether they are fair. We may conclude that a rule is unfair, and change it going forward. But we don't change the rules to fit the situation. We can't have it one way for one person and another way for another person.

Certainly, there have been times when someone has a strong argument for making an exception to the rules. While I may have compassion for someone's difficult circumstances, we must draw the line and abide by the rules. There are things that happen to our people that you wish didn't happen. This is why we have policies and procedures. Everything is clearly and concisely spelled out so there are no misunderstandings. Everyone knows the rules beforehand.

Even today, a consultant sometimes calls me to say, I missed making the incentive trip because this happened and that happened. "It's just not fair, Doris, you just have to bend the rules."

My pat answer is, "No, we can't bend the rules. Our job is to make sure that the rules are fair and clearly stated. Now, if we made a mistake, if we haven't given you what you need to know to compete on a fair basis, then we have to consider that. But if we've told you the rules, they are the same rules that everybody has. If we think, as a company, that those rules are not fair going forward, we might do something about changing them. But right now, they are the rules and everybody competes in the same way."

Susie Lite, one of our Sales Managers, worked for six years in the sales field. As she puts it, "I've been there and I've experienced the Consultants' challenges. When a Consultant misses an important goal and an incentive trip because her Kitchen Show didn't make the deadline, I tell her, 'I know from personal experience what you're going through. I know there is nothing I can say today to make you feel any better. But what I can do to help you overcome your disappointment is to look at it for what it is so we can move on and build from here. I've been here since

1989, and no matter what level you are, it doesn't matter whether you can tell a better story or cry bigger tears. Everyone is treated fairly. There is no favoritism. This is one of the company's biggest strengths. Can you imagine what would happen if the company made an exception for one person but not someone else? She'd think, "Oh great. My story was just as compelling as hers was. Why did the company make an exception for her but not me?" '

"There is comfort in knowing we have the same rules for everyone," Susie says. "I might not satisfy a Consultant's immediate problem, but she will respect the company's position and its integrity.

" 'Now instead of letting this defeat you,' I told the Consultant, ending on a positive note, 'I'll tell you what I did when I was struggling to put a booking on the calendar. I knew what I had to do. I had to pick up the phone. Do what you have to do and I predict that there will be many incentive trips in your future.' "

I believe The Pampered Chef is a stronger company today because our field people are aware we have specific rules that we stand behind. People have to know the rules are on solid footing, not shifting sand.

VEXING VENDORS

Depending on one's point of view, it is either a disadvantage or an advantage that we have never manufactured our own products. The downside is that when we were a small company, we didn't get a lot of respect from some of our suppliers. They were unwilling to custom-make products to meet our specifications, they refused to give us exclusivity on products we designed, and they tried to sell us products we didn't want. We also had to deal with a lot of manufacturers as a small account, sometimes buying only one or two products. They accused us of "cherry picking" and some tried to jam products down our throat that we didn't want. Simply put, they didn't understand our business.

We believe that the upside has far outweighed the downside. Manufacturing our own products would have required large sums of capital, which would have curtailed our growth. The costs of materials, manufacturing facilities, and equipment would have been enormous. So while we invested in inventory, technology, and distribution centers, we didn't have manufacturing costs. In addition to being highly capital-intensive, manufacturing is highly labor-intensive. Because we lacked capital, we didn't have a choice in manufacturing our own kitchen tools. It wasn't even an option. Our focus was on finding companies willing to make our products. If it came to the point that one company couldn't supply our demand, we'd find an additional company. Fortunately, plenty of vendors out there wanted our business—we just had to find them.

Manufacturers were accustomed to doing business with retailers such as hardware stores, department stores, and specialty stores. These retailers bought the manufacturer's entire line and frequently promoted its brand. Our vendors didn't understand that my product line strategy was to selectively offer kitchen tools that provided high-quality value and functionality to our customers. It was our wide selection of products not available from any other single source that contributed to our uniqueness at a Kitchen Show. Some manufacturers became angry when we'd buy one or two items from them and others from a competing brand. It was akin to a restaurant selling Coca-Cola and Diet Pepsi. If you sell Coca-Cola, you can't sell Diet Pepsi, and vice versa.

Of course, when we were buying only a single item from a

housewares manufacturer, we were an unimportant customer, and were treated accordingly. To many, we were a nuisance account. Later, when we did huge volumes with a single item, manufacturers began to pay more attention to us. Even then, the salesman's mentality was, "If The Pampered Chef can sell thousands of this one item, just think what they could sell if I could get them to carry twenty-five of our products." This is when we'd spar back and forth. Frankly, due to my inexperience, I didn't understand where they were coming from. However, I was very clear on what I was doing. It boiled down to the fact that we were operating on totally different parameters.

As the volume of our orders became more substantial, I asked manufacturers for exclusive rights to sell a particular item. They flatly refused. Again, I didn't have a clear understanding of their business; from their point of view, they had accounts with many retailers, and they weren't willing to risk upsetting them. To them, it seemed preposterous to pull an item from their existing product line strictly to benefit us. Once I realized this, we started to design products according to our own specifications, and asked manufacturers to make them exclusively for us. Gradually, some manufacturers consented.

Leifheit, the prominent German company, was one of our top manufacturers. We carried several of their products. At the time we were selling an egg slicer made by another German company, and Leifheit asked us to sell theirs instead.

"I think we can sell a lot of your slicers," I told them, "but we want you to make it based on our specs. And we want an exclusive on it."

"That's not possible," I was told. "We can't do that for you."

So I found a domestic company that agreed to produce it according to our specs, which included a removable blade and making the egg slicer dishwasher safe. When a Leifheit representative saw it in our catalog, the company approached me and asked, "Why didn't you let us make this for you?"

"There are a couple of reasons," I replied. "First is price, and second, you were unwilling to give it to us exclusively."

I have to give them credit for the turnabout they did in handling our account. After that, they agreed to work with us on certain exclusive products, and since then we've had some fairly complex products made to our specs by Leifheit. These products have done well, and over the years Leifheit has added more items to our product line manufactured exclusively for us.

Other manufacturers flat out say, "We're not going to do anything exclusive with you," or "You can have this model only in your market." As a result, we have contracted out some custom-made products to companies in the Pacific Rim, in particular Taiwan and China. Leifheit basically told us, "We are not going to make you go to the Far East. We see value in doing business with you." Our relationship with them epitomizes the beautiful collaboration possible between two companies. I think of it as a win-win situation. We collaborate on the design of some of our most important products. They provide expert engineering and manufacturing—we then sell the product through our sales network.

Another important business lesson we learned: we stick to our knitting. We do what we know how to do, and we find other companies skilled in manufacturing. It would be presumptuous for us to think we could manufacture several hundred products in a wide range of materials and manufacturing processes with the same quality the top-rated companies that serve as our vendors do. Had we strayed, I am certain either the quality or the variety of our product line would have suffered, and our business would have not been as financially successful.

VENDORS WHO LIKED US BETTER WHEN WE WERE SMALL

Speaking of growing pains, I was surprised to discover that some vendors reacted negatively when our small orders became big orders.

When I was a student, every member of the graduating class of the School of Home Economics at the University of Illinois received an apple wedger as a graduation gift from the Apple Growers Association. When pressed down, this unusual kitchen tool wedges fruit such as apples and pears into eight sections; it also removes the core. Back then, some food manufacturers courted graduating home economics students much as drug companies today do medical students. I used this wedger in my own kitchen and over the years immensely enjoyed it. Fifteen years later when I started The Pampered Chef, I thought this would be an apt product to include in our product line. The name of the company that manufactured it was stamped on the apple wedger, and after doing my homework, I called the owner, who operated a small factory in Kenosha, Wisconsin.

After explaining how I came upon the wedger, and how much I used it over the years, I asked, "Are you still making it?"

"Our core business is metal fabrications," he answered with a thick German accent, "but, yes, we still make the wedger."

So he agreed to sell it to us. I was delighted. Over the years, he called a few times and would say to me, "What are you guys doing with our wedgers? Are you giving it away? I've never had anybody order so many."

His factory wasn't far from Chicago, and on occasion I'd mention that we would like to tour his factory. Each time, he'd give an excuse why we shouldn't come. "We're such a tiny operation," he often apologized. "There's nothing here for you to see."

As we grew, we kept ordering more and more. One day he

called and said, "I'm sorry, Doris, but you're buying too many from me; I can't make that many for you."

The holiday season was approaching and I became quite concerned. "Can you sub out the work to another company?" I asked.

"I'm sorry, Doris, but this is how many I can make for you in a year. I can't supply you with additional units until next year."

"Let's try to work together and figure this out," I said.

"I can't do any more; I won't do any more," he insisted. "I don't want the increase."

"If your nine-to-five shift can't produce more wedgers for us, won't you consider having your people work overtime to accommodate us?"

"Nope."

"How about having a second shift make additional units in the evenings or on weekends?"

"Can't do it," he answered.

I tried explaining that we needed enough inventory to fill every order we received. "We won't be buying any from you if we can't have wedgers for all of our customers who place orders," I explained. I told him how many we anticipated selling during the current year, and I explained that the following year the order would increase, and our order would be even greater the next year, and the year after.

"Why don't you understand the word 'no'?" he asked.

"You leave us no alternative but to find somebody else to make wedgers for us."

"That's fine. Do that," he said abruptly, ending the conversation. So that's what we did.

A similar incident occurred with a St. Louis company that made a line of kitchen tools, including a wonderful handheld can opener. We carried it for years, recognizing that it was the gold standard for can openers. In 1990, it was one of our hottest products, and we anticipated it would be a major item for the coming fall holiday season. We contacted the company and announced our plans to increase our original order for can openers. The account manager told us, "We're sorry, but that's it for this season. We are not scheduled to manufacture any more until early next year."

I called personally to talk to the company's owner. "We've been selling a fairly large number of your can openers, and we don't want to disappoint our customers. Surely you can help us find a way to work this out."

"There isn't anything we can do. I'm sorry, ma'am."

"If you can't make more for us, is it possible that you can find them for us somewhere else?"

"No. Absolutely not."

"You might consider calling some of your accounts that have them in stock, and if it's a poor seller for them, perhaps we can buy what they have in inventory," I pleaded. "You'll be performing a service for them, as well as helping us."

"There is nothing we can do," he insisted.

It was apparent to me that this was one company that was not going to grow with us. I said to our people, "Okay, that's it for them. We need to take those products out of our line until we find another source."

Today, the apple wedger and the can opener are made by different manufacturers. We found companies there that were willing to do back bends to accommodate us.

BUSINESS TRIPS TO THE FAR EAST

I first started going to the Far East in the late 1980s. The trips were exhausting, particularly because on those early trips I couldn't afford to fly business class. Flying in coach was quite an experience; the plane was often crowded with Chinese nationals and Taiwanese nationals who didn't speak English. Families passed food with delicious aromas back and forth, up and down the aisles. One man who sat in my row on a return flight had apparently never flown before. He didn't know how to undo his seatbelt; as I watched in astonishment, he stood up on his seat and stepped out of his seatbelt before walking matter-of-factly down the aisle toward the washroom.

On one of my first trips to the Far East, I met with a Japanese manufacturer that made a pizza cutter and a garnisher for us. My Japanese agent accompanied me to the company's headquarters; I sat across a large conference table facing several executives. I was the only woman in the room; after everyone respectfully handed me a business card, I was virtually ignored. Nobody bothered to speak English other than my agent, who was my translator. I had wanted to meet with them to request modifications in their pizza cutter. The entire meeting was conducted in Japanese, and at one point the men around the table had a twenty-minute discussion. I sat politely, waiting for it to conclude. When I asked my agent what was said, he gave me a fifteen-second explanation in English. I wanted to jump up and say, "Who is the customer here?" What I did was arrange all of their business cards in front of me, according to where they sat at the conference table. While they were talking among themselves, I memorized each of their names; at the end of the meeting, I said "Thank you" in Japanese, shaking each of their hands and calling them by their correct name with the proper pronunciation. No matter how I was treated abroad, I was determined to do my best to be a goodwill ambassador for the United States. I did, however, change agents.

By the late 1980s, the Japanese were building wonderful high-tech products; they seemed to have lost interest in making the kinds of products we carry. So I took some items to Taiwan to shop around for new manufacturers. One Taiwan manufacturer that we chose to do our work was unable to make the garnisher or pizza cutter according to our specifications. They kept trying for a year and a half, but were unable to get it right. For some reason, they couldn't properly make a rippled blade. They also had difficulty with the handle on the garnish cutter, a thin, U-shaped piece of metal that is wrinkled. They tried to cut it at the top of the horseshoe and then put a handle over it, but that way, it lost its strength and stability. These were major products for us. After several trips to Taiwan and countless attempts to get it right, the manufacturers finally succeeded in meeting our specs, and we began to import the pizza cutter and garnisher from them. The point is, however, that unlike the Japanese, the Taiwanese were eager to accommodate me. They took me on tours of their factories and treated me as if I were a queen. More important, they did whatever was necessary to please us and our customers.

Over the years, we've requested several improvements to these two products. With the pizza cutter my goal was to have a cutter that was sharpened on both sides of the wheel, made of stainless steel throughout. It was a matter of making product improvements again and again, always looking for new and better ways of achieving our specs. It can be very time-consuming and exhausting; I'd sometimes make as many as four or five trips a year to the Far East. However, our products require getting involved in the nitty-gritty of the design and manufacturing and I loved to do it.

THE FREEZE

Although Jay and I were accustomed to working long hours, the summer of 1990 was particularly busy. Business was booming. When Labor Day weekend arrived, it was a welcome breather. Jay and I used the three-day weekend to review our inventory and make projections for the coming fall and holiday season, our busiest time of year. As we periodically did, we took a close look at the products in our warehouse and what inventory was coming in the door.

We also reviewed the sizable increase in the number of agreements with Kitchen Consultants we'd made, a good barometer to project sales volume. During the year, several positive articles in national publications about The Pampered Chef resulted in our being swamped with inquiries from people wanting to attend Kitchen Shows and wanting to become Consultants.

"Look at the number of Consultant agreements that came in this past quarter," Jay exclaimed. "All that publicity . . ."

"Our recruiting numbers are off the charts," I said. "We're up nearly four hundred percent from last year."

"We're growing strong in our heartland," Jay said, referring to the Chicago area and the surrounding states. "And we're also getting people from new areas of the country."

"Are you thinking what I'm thinking?" I asked Jay. "How are we going to get the orders out and have sufficient inventory to stock new ones?"

"We could run into a real problem with product if this trend continues," Jay answered, concerned.

Admittedly, our forecasting was unsophisticated; but we did have enough of a handle on our business to see the handwriting on the wall. We were well aware we could not withstand a lot of back order. If the company was unable to satisfy orders, we'd risk alienating our Consultants, hostesses, and ultimately our customers. It would be a disaster. If the company ran out of stock on multiple items, it would devastate morale in the field. We decided that our number one objective was to prevent that kind of crash in inventory. Could we simply acquire more inventory? No, not at this time of year. Manufacturers were low on inventory, and some would soon be shutting down their factories until after the first of the year. We could not rely on increasing our inventories to meet demand for our products. Nor did we have the capacity to crank out a far greater number of orders from our inadequate warehouse space. And since we processed orders manually, we had limitations on handling higher sales volumes.

"This is a serious dilemma, but it's a short-term problem," Jay said thoughtfully. "In time, we can obtain more inventory, we can bring in more people, and we can get more space. But it's going to take time. Meanwhile, we're coming to our strongest sales period—September through mid-December."

"Jay, you're so good at putting things in perspective," I said with a relieved sigh. "Come January, we'll have some breathing room. We've got to focus on getting through the next four months."

"So here's where we are," Jay said. "We can't turn up our distribution capability or our inventory at the snap of a finger. We have no control in these areas. But what we *can* control is the number of Consultants, and orders, coming in."

"This is a relationship business," I pointed out. "Many of the people in the field have been busy recruiting Consultants for the past several weeks. Many are probably in the process of making a decision to become Pampered Chef Consultants as we speak. If we put a freeze on accepting Consultant agreements, it's going to be a problem in the field."

"You're right. In the direct-sales industry, a recruiting freeze could be the kiss of death," Jay cautioned. "We're enjoying tremendous momentum. Do we want to risk stopping or reversing that momentum? Putting a hold on recruiting will wreak havoc in the field."

"On the other hand, Jay, it's the one thing we can control. If our infrastructure can't support our sales volume, we have to cut back somewhere."

I talked to several DSA members. Most advised against instituting a recruiting freeze. "You'll kill the goose that lays the golden egg," one warned. Another cautioned, "Nobody puts a hold on recruiting. That's signing your own death warrant." But in the end, it didn't matter what outsiders told us. We knew that if we were unable to handle the business in December, we could implode. With our reputation tarnished, it would be very difficult to get it back.

After carefully reviewing our options, Jay and I decided to communicate a detailed explanation of our predicament to the sales organization. We spent the next three days scrutinizing our decision with our management team, then we drafted a letter. On the Friday after Labor Day weekend, we published the following letter in *Consultant News*, our monthly publication distributed to our sales organization:

September 7, 1990

Dear Consultants,

The incredible growth we have experienced over the past several months is evident to us at the home office on a national scale, and I know you are seeing it in your own clusters. Growth is positive, and will ultimately bring countless benefits to our Consultants and customers in the form of better products, systems and service. Growth, however, needs to be managed. That is the subject of this letter.

In order to manage our growth and to provide optimum service to our Consultants and our customers,

*we are placing the following carefully thought-out
plan into action:*

Action #1: Temporary Recruiting "Hold"

*We will put a temporary recruiting
"hold" into effect beginning October 1,
1990. Our expectation is that this will
extend until January 1, 1991. We will
accept Consultant agreements from now
through noon October 1, 1990. No new
agreements will be accepted after that date
until further notice.*

*Reason: August 1990 resulted in close to
a 400% increase in the number of new
Consultant agreements over the same month
last year. This follows a very strong previous
six months of recruiting. We are instituting
the "hold" in order to assure a quality level
of service to our existing Consultants for the
remainder of 1990. We are doing this in
order to support you as you develop your
Pampered Chef business now and for the
future. The "hold" will also allow us to shift
human resources away from the process of
enrolling new Consultants and shipping kits
and into other areas of our operation for the
busy fall season.*

Action #2: Cut-off Date for Christmas Delivery Orders

*The cut-off date for promised
Christmas delivery of "in stock"*

*merchandise will be orders received in the
home office by noon November 2, 1990.
Orders received in the home office beyond
that date will be accepted without a
guaranteed Christmas delivery.*

Many companies today, both inside and outside our
industry, are facing weak or declining sales. That is not
our challenge.

We have a great opportunity to grow and develop
into a huge force with incredible growth in the '90s.
The situation is at the same time both a delight—and
a challenge.

The actions I have outlined in this letter are necessary. After much deliberation, our management team
believes these are the right choices. They reflect prudent
management that will move us into 1991 and beyond
as a stable, solid company that you can depend on.

In order to prepare ourselves for future growth
and success, we must be willing to accept challenges
along the way. By working together and understanding
each other's needs and concerns, there should be no
obstacle we cannot overcome!

Best regards,
Doris K. Christopher
President

For the most part, my letter was well received by our sales
organization. Certainly, it upset some people, because this action temporarily limited their ability to advance in the business.
There were others who concluded that something was drastically

wrong with the company. I realized that to reach out to everyone I'd have to meet personally with people. Normally, this time of year, I do not travel, but that fall I met with every Director, and attended at least one monthly meeting of their cluster. I wanted to make sure they could see, face to face, that everything was okay. I explained that we understood that they were inconvenienced. "However, what we were doing is better than the alternative—disappointing our customers and our Consultants by not having enough product for them," I emphasized.

"We are doing our best," I explained to everyone. "We are a small company, and we are growing quickly. But we have to temporarily slow things down; we'll work closely with you in this unusual situation. We ask for your faith in the company and our management team. Together, we can pull this off."

By the time the recruiting freeze went into effect, our Consultants accepted it. They continued to recruit, explaining that all prospective Consultants would be placed on a waiting list, and after the first of the year they would have an opportunity to join our organization.

It's interesting how things worked out. As expected, the field had grumbled, but when the freeze was lifted early the next year, there was a tremendous surge of Consultant contracts submitted. Our momentum picked up again as if it had never been interrupted. To this day, people say to me, "Do you remember the waiting list back in 1990? I was on it." In some ways, the freeze enhanced our recruiting efforts; people desire things all the more that are hard to get. Jay compares it to being put on a waiting list for acceptance by a prestigious college.

Looking back, the recruiting freeze augmented our reputation with our sales force, customers, and vendors. People saw us as an honest company that was trying to do the right thing and not overestimate its capabilities. We are very conservative in our business practices by nature, and our people knew that. When we told them something, they knew it was the truth. Of the 1,200 people on the recruiting list, relatively few failed to sign Consultant contracts when the freeze was lifted.

One of the people we hired into the home office during the freeze was Linda Stupar, who had done order processing with two direct-sales companies. She was a stay-at-home mom with a daughter in kindergarten. Linda had sent her résumé to us in 1988, but I had tucked it away, unable to justify such a hire. Then in September 1990 I called her. "You sent us your résumé a while back," I said to her. "We're looking for someone like you to lead our order processing." Following an interview, Linda started immediately.

We were still processing our orders manually. Linda had experience in processing orders via computers, so we brought her in to convert the rest of the staff. "It was a real challenge getting people to see computers as a better and faster way to process orders," Linda admits.

Before converting to computers, our cutoff date for Christmas delivery, as you'll remember, was November 2. Today our cutoff date is mid-December, a testament to the effectiveness of the systems we put in place.

It had taken us seven years to hit the $1 million mark in sales, and only three years to go from $1 million to $10 million. In February 1991, we moved our headquarters from 344 Lathrop to a 40,000-square-foot facility at 205 Fencl Lane in Hillside, in anticipation of continued growth.

Our forecast proved correct. We recorded over $20 million in sales in 1991. The following year, to handle additional volume, we added another facility at 150 Fencl Lane, giving us a total of 70,000 square feet (with the warehouse at 7771 Van Buren that we bought in 1991). Our 1992 sales nearly doubled again that year, exceeding $38 million. In 1994, we moved to another new facility at 350 South Rohlwing Road in Addison, signing a five-year lease for half the space in a 450,000-square-foot building. We thought that space would be more than enough through 1999. Two years later, we signed a lease for the entire building. In 1996, we opened an additional warehouse at 500 East Kehoe in Carol Stream.

In 1998 our annual sales surpassed the $500 million mark. In 2000 we moved into two additional buildings, one that housed our customer service and order processing departments, and the other that gave us much-needed additional warehousing space. By this point, we had 60,000 Kitchen Consultants conducting Pampered Chef Kitchen Shows in the United States, Canada, the United Kingdom, and Germany. By 2001 that number had grown to 67,000 Consultants worldwide and 1,100 home-office Co-workers. The year 2002 marked the celebration of our grand opening in our new international headquarters at One Pampered Chef Lane in Addison, a 780,000-square-foot building that con-solidates our home office and warehouse under one roof. We now have over twenty acres of space. Three hundred houses the size of the Christopher home where we started the business could fit in this building.

Our new building is spacious, with 600,000 square feet of warehouse and thirty-eight-foot ceilings, enabling us to stack goods higher.

Over the years, we've had our share of moving days. We're old hands at it. Before moving into our second building on Lath-rop Avenue, we hired Corwin Will, a schoolteacher who moon-lighted to supplement his teaching salary, as our remodeling contractor. Corwin and his wife were good friends of ours. A jack-of-all-trades, Corwin took down some walls and added others to the building and also did plumbing and electrical work.

When we moved into our building on Van Buren, we contracted him again, to take an empty warehouse and convert it to a warehouse with offices. He installed conveyors for our pick-and-pack system, a first. We also added pallet racks and a forklift, another first for the company.

We were so pleased with Corwin's work that we hired him as our operations manager. He also served as facilities manager, responsible for the day-to-day operations and for the maintenance of all the mechanical systems, from equipment to the heating and air-conditioning. This was typical at The Pampered Chef at the time—everyone wore several hats. We all worked hard, putting in whatever hours were required to get the work done.

"We were always fortunate during this period of enormous growth," Corwin explains, "to have the luxury of setting up the new building with new equipment. So once the building was ready, our people packed their personal belongings on Friday, and by Monday morning they went to the new building and were back on the job, virtually without missing a beat. With all these moves, we rarely had a glitch or interruption in service. We just kept putting the orders out."

Our new building is spacious enough that we believe we can handle sizable increases in sales volume before we outgrow it. But as you've just read, we've been wrong on our predictions before. Who knows?

7
You Win with People

A woman who owned a small direct-sales company once asked me, "How did you know when to relinquish certain responsibilities to others? I'd like to know, Doris, because my company is now at that stage where I'm struggling with when I should delegate."

We grew so fast in the 1990s, I really had no choice. It wasn't an option. I couldn't possibly have made all the decisions. I wasn't able to do everything myself anymore. We were growing at a rapid pace, and one thing you don't want to do with a direct-selling company is cap its momentum.

It didn't take me long to figure out that there were people who knew more than I did about many areas of my business. My strong suits were not finance, warehousing, distribution, or technology. This meant that I had to find good people in these areas and be careful not to hold anyone back. To do this, we had to choose individuals with sound understanding in their areas— managers we felt had excellent skills—so we could turn them loose, trusting they would do well.

Although our business grew by leaps and bounds, we were no overnight success story. In the beginning, we grew one person at a time. We made sure to pick people we could be comfortable with. That's because we were a very small operation, and the people we hired would work with us in close quarters, day in and day out. So we selected people who would be compatible. Still, with a limited budget, we had little depth, so we couldn't afford to make mistakes in our selection of people. This also meant we were very dependent on each person to carry his or her weight. We wanted individuals who would be hardworking, who had integrity and would be loyal to our company.

In the beginning, everyone multitasked. Throughout the 1980s, I was known to do a quick change of clothes from a business outfit to a pair of jeans and sweatshirt, to lend a hand in picking and packing orders. Yes, I wore many hats, but I wasn't the only one who did.

We were a close-knit group. We were all on a first-name basis. If somebody ever called me "Mrs. Christopher," I'd set them straight. "Please call me Doris." (Although we've grown from a handful of home-office people to close to one thousand, I'm still Doris and Jay is still Jay.) Because we worked so closely with everyone, it didn't take us long to size up a prospective employee. As the company grew, it became necessary to delegate more and more responsibilities, but we knew our people well enough to know what we could expect of them. I believe this is true with any company—when you're close to your business, you are better able to evaluate people and judge whether they are capable of moving to the next level. This would not be true with absentee management.

Certainly there have been people with The Pampered Chef who have not been able to move on to the next level. Co-workers have left because they felt uncomfortable working for an organization to which they were unable to contribute. Then too, there have been some people who have been good at a certain stage of the company's development, but at a later stage their personal growth didn't keep up with the company's growth. This is where tough decisions have to be made. At times, technology has eliminated jobs held by good people. Thankfully, the company was experiencing tremendous growth, which allowed us to find slots to place these people in other areas. As a result, many good people have jobs in areas different from where they initially started.

In 1994, after working full time at The Pampered Chef since 1987, Jay left the company. He now runs Thatcher Corporation, a successful consulting firm that specializes in technology-related services. It had always been our plan that Jay would move on to run his own business, and in 1994 the timing was good. In the eight years Jay had been here full time, our sales went from $1 million to $135 million! We had several key managers in place by that time. Jay still serves on The Pampered Chef's board of directors, and will always be my closest confidant.

GENERAL PRINCIPLES ON HIRING PEOPLE

Frequently, Jay is asked to lecture on entrepreneurship at local colleges. One of his favorite topics is hiring employees, elucidating the principles we espouse based on hiring practices we learned over the years in our business. These principles are:

- *Hire good people.* Hire to the highest standards you can, and as quickly as you can. Pay the extra money to get the best person. Don't beat around the bush saying, "This person could fill in and he'll do an okay job." You're not looking for people to do an okay job. You're looking for people who can do an exceptional job. This is not a place to cut corners.

- *Check references.* Make sure applicants are who they represent themselves to be. Contact past employers and co-workers. Do your homework—a small company cannot afford to have a bad apple!
- *Every person counts.* A small organization can't have a weak link, so you must hire the strongest people available.
- *Give them responsibility with authority.* Remember that people don't like being dictated to. When people with experience and creativity are hired, let them use it. Give them the freedom to run with the ball.
- *Review and evaluate.* People want feedback on how they are doing. One of the roles of management is to provide them with guidance so they can become even better employees for your company. While most companies evaluate people on an annual basis, we suggest that you do it more frequently with new people: consider a ninety-day review to make sure they're on the right track. Here, you can communicate with them on your expectations, and whether they are meeting those expectations.

In our early years, we were not able to compete with the going rate bigger companies paid for good people. We couldn't follow suit and remain profitable. Nor was it in our game plan to attract people by giving away ownership in our business, as some companies do. Consequently, we didn't get some of the people we wanted. To attract good people, we had to convince them that this was a good organization with great growth potential, that there would be opportunities to succeed and grow as the company did.

We've always had a good reputation within the direct-selling industry. Good people came to us through word of mouth. Our staff also helped us attract good people as they told their friends about us. Still other good people had been exposed to the company via Kitchen Shows.

THE COMPANY GROWS ONLY AS OUR PEOPLE GROW

As our company grew, there was a corresponding growth in our people. It can't happen any other way. Perhaps nobody grew more than I.

When I made my first trips to the Merchandise Mart during the summer of 1980, I was green as an apple. The moment I opened my mouth in a manufacturer's showroom, it was clear I had no business experience.

As my tiny business grew step by step, so did I. In business terms, I had to learn like a small child, first to crawl, then slowly to walk and to run. Jay's business acumen was far superior to mine; never in my wildest dreams did I imagine I'd be as knowledgeable and astute as he was. Jay, as my teacher and mentor, also has had enormous growth. His business knowledge in 1980 pales in comparison to what he knows today.

Initially, Jay and I worked closely together as a team. As our company grew, we hardly noticed that we, too, were growing and learning. It was an exhilarating time.

Even more exhilarating was seeing our people grow. Had they not, our small company would have died on the vine. We didn't build The Pampered Chef without a lot of help from many others.

Because we couldn't compete with large corporations, we were unable to recruit high-echelon executives with proven track records. We were, however, able to hire young, talented middle managers who had not yet risen to executive suite status. By diligently picking and choosing the right people, we recruited a team of men and women whom we believed were up-and-comers—individuals who could grow with us. Our facilities manager, Corwin Will, was one such example. During our 2002 move into our vast new headquarters and warehouse, Corwin remarked, "Just five years ago, I would not have considered tackling such an undertaking. But I had the advantage of having made all those previous Pampered Chef moves. It got to the point that each time we relocated, it was already time to plan for the next building. After the last couple of moves, I wasn't intimidated by the huge open space because I had dealt with it before on a smaller scale."

Rick Geu, our Executive Vice President and Chief Financial Officer, joined the company in 1992. His background included a four-year stint with Price Waterhouse, as well as seventeen years at Lien Chemical Company, where he met Jay, and three years at By Design, Inc., a landscape architecture firm based in Chicago. "Watching from afar," Rick says, "I witnessed that it took seven years for The Pampered Chef to hit the one-million-dollar mark, and then just four more for sales to jump to twenty million. So when I joined, I expected to see a lot of growth. But nothing like what has actually happened. It got to the point during my first few years here that when we'd make growth projections, our rule of thumb was to double our sales over the previous year. Look at the numbers: we went from $20.5 million in 1991 to $38 million in 1992, $69 million in 1993, $135.5 million in 1994, and $224 million in 1995. In 1996 we did $330 million, $426 million in 1997, and $500 million in 1998.

"But did I imagine in 1992 that I'd be the CFO for a company geared to do a billion dollars?" Rick asks. "Had the company been its present size when I was working for the landscape architecture firm, I wouldn't have felt qualified to be its CFO. Like everyone else around here, I grew into my job."

When I first interviewed Rick Geu, I talked to him about the internal controls and the checks and balances we needed to put in place. As Rick admits, "When I came here, there were no internal controls or checks and balances. There were no written procedures or documentation. The company didn't have purchase orders or receiving orders. There were no timely financial statements. The company was growing so fast back then that they never took the time to do those things."

His primary responsibility was to develop these controls, procedures, and the documentation from ground zero, in order to make sure everything that got shipped was actually paid for, and that nothing went out the door that shouldn't have. In short, his job was to put controls in place to safeguard the company's assets, and to do it without direction from me.

Another key person to join us that same year was Ralph VanDyke, our manager of computer operations. After serving in the U.S. Navy as a data systems specialist for six years, Ralph worked at Children's Hospital in its IT Data Center on the third shift. "Linda Stupar sat in with me during the interview," Jay says, "and we were quite impressed with Ralph."

"When will you be available to start?" Jay asked Ralph.

"I can start today. But I'll have to call my wife," he said.

"We're not going to give your coat back to you until she says you can stay," Jay kidded him.

I liked Ralph's sense of humor. He was on the job by midday, hours after we had first met. At the time, there were only a few PCs in the entire company. When Ralph started, he was a one-man shop. Our Information Services department now employs eighty people. As our need for information services grew, Ralph's job grew. Today, under his supervision, a staff of twenty is responsible for operating our telecommunications, networking, systems administration, and technical training, as well as running our production and report distribution jobs.

Rich Schubkegel joined our company as Information Services Vice President in 1996. Rich had worked for a micro-imaging software company and was formerly employed as Director of Computer Systems for the Evanston-Skokie School District, and before that with Lotus Software Company. Today every department in the entire organization depends on IS; because we host our own Web sites, every consultant and customer can link on to us. This is quite a contrast to the early days when Consultants' orders came by mail written down on a piece of paper that had to be keyed to our data-processing system. When we started our program back in 1995, there was no Internet for the general public to link on to; it was just a modem-to-modem transfer. Today, our Consultants can transmit orders to us over the Internet, or by accessing our virtual private network.

"The cost to process an order by paper used to be $4.17," Rich explains. "But when we process it electronically, it's down to about twenty-one cents. And although we've continued to grow by fifty to a hundred percent a year, our order-processing department hasn't had to keep adding staff. In fact, through natural attrition, we've actually been able to reduce staff."

Corwin Will, Rick Geu, Ralph VanDyke, and Rich Schubkegel are only four of the exceptional people who have enjoyed tremendous personal growth since joining the company. When our people grow, we grow.

WE ARE FAMILY

During my first years in business, I intimately knew everyone who worked for The Pampered Chef. Not only did I know every Consultant, I frequently knew the names of their spouses and their children. Of course that's possible only with a small company. Today, I am unable to have the same personal relationships with everyone. While the numbers have changed, our family values remain intact. They are deeply ingrained in the culture.

Early on, I wrote personal handwritten notes to accompany monthly commission checks. I called everyone on birthdays, anniversaries, and during the holiday season. This isn't possible today. But I still send a birthday card to every Director, and notes or cards for other important life occasions, like births, deaths, and illnesses, and flowers with a card to upper-level Directors. I also send flowers to every upper-level director who is promoted. Our focus is and always will be on the family. This is who we are.

THE PERSONAL TOUCH

Ours is a personal business. A Kitchen Consultant is invited to a host's home to be with her friends and family members. The setting of a Kitchen Show is not a business environment; it's a social gathering, with people getting together around the dining room or kitchen table, enjoying good company and eating good food. The conversation is focused on preparing meals for the family. Our business was built on personal relationships, ever since my first Kitchen Show, when I was the guest of a friend, who in turn invited her friends to come.

The personal touch is the small businessperson's biggest advantage over big companies. It is the reason why there will always be successful small companies that won't be driven out of business by giant corporations. Nobody can treat a customer the way the owner of a company can. In our business each of our Consultants is an independent businessperson. Yet each Consultant is a goodwill ambassador for The Pampered Chef as well; how he or she conducts business is a direct reflection on the company. In most instances, the Consultant is the only contact a customer has with the company. A Consultant's relationship with customers is personal. This is an advantage many other companies don't have. I think of it as the crucial edge that small companies have over big companies.

Let me give you an example. When you walk into a restaurant and the owner personally greets you, it's the kind of welcome that nobody else can give you. Perhaps the owner even calls you by name. If the service is substandard, a restaurant owner can pick up the tab, give you a free dessert, or comp your meal on your next visit. When the owner thanks you for your patronage, it's as if the whole business is thanking you. That's because he or she is the business. The same is true when you walk into a small retail store. I know how good I feel when the owner of a clothing boutique greets me, "You know, Doris, recently, I was thinking about you. A new outfit just arrived, and it's the perfect color for you, and it's also your size. While you're looking around, let me get it for you."

When companies expand, it's not always possible for the owner to extend this same kind of personal service. A restaurant owner with two locations can't welcome every customer because he can't be at two places at the same time. The bigger a restaurant chain or a retail chain grows, the less it can depend on the owner's personal touch to please customers. But what a business owner can do is make sure her people have been properly trained to bend over backward for customers. To do this, an owner must lead by example, so her employees will emulate her behavior. Only then will her warmth and caring permeate the organization and reach the customers and vendors.

It is no longer possible for me to greet all Consultants or all Co-workers by name as I once did. I do, however, give a warm, personal greeting to everyone I see at the home office and at the conference. I say hello to everyone who passes by in the halls of our building, including visitors. In doing so, as the company leader, I believe I'm setting an example for everyone else. Our building is a friendly place to work. I visited one large company where the founder-CEO is reserved and rather cold. His aloofness is duplicated throughout the organization. People rarely say hello in hallways, on elevators, or in the dining area. His company has an executive dining room that excludes practically all employees with the exception of a few senior people. His company's treatment of employees is based on position. I believe in treating all people with respect, regardless of their rank. I don't approve of companies having private dining rooms because it dampens the morale of those denied entry. Besides, a company eating area occupied by employees at all levels is a great place to fraternize. When Jay eats in the building, he routinely sits down with different groups of Co-workers.

"It's a great way to get ideas from them in an informal setting," he says, "and it's always good to get to know people away from their offices. By talking to them about their families, their hobbies, and so forth, I often pick up something about them that explains a lot about who they are. I listen to their thoughts and comments on nonbusiness subjects; as a result, they know I care for them as human beings, not just as people who work for the company. I don't judge who they are by the job they have or how much they make. Anyone, with any job, can be a wonderful mother and homemaker. She may be a leader in her church, a volunteer for the American Cancer Society, and so on. Who they are is not defined just by their work. When I worked at The Pampered Chef full time, I'd sit down at a different table every day. I did it because I wanted to know our people—really know them."

Both Jay and I are good listeners. As somebody once said to me, "If God wanted us to talk more than we listen, He would have given us two mouths and only one ear." Listening to people—I mean really listening—is a sign that you respect the other person's opinion. It means you think he or she has something worthwhile to say. I've always believed that any person who works at a job eight hours a day has a good understanding of that job. The best solutions to internal problems can be found by your own people. Don't be shy about asking them for their opinions. Not only will they feel good about themselves because you came to them for their advice, you'll also find solutions that otherwise might not have surfaced.

Well-managed companies create a working atmosphere where people feel comfortable approaching management with ideas, because they know their ideas will be heard. We have an open-door policy that lets our Co-workers know they are welcome to meet with senior executives if they have an issue to talk over. If there are problems they want to discuss with me, I want them to feel comfortable in my presence. To make people feel at ease, I avoid sitting behind my desk when someone is in my office. Today, I have a conference room off my office where I meet with people. This way, I don't have a desk that could serve as a barrier. Before the conference room, I walked around from behind my desk to greet visitors and pulled up a chair across from them so we could chat informally. And depending on my role at a meeting, I'm just as likely to sit on the side at the middle of the table as I am to sit at the head. It's my preference for the person who is leading the meeting to be at the place where he or she can be seen and heard—not me.

CO-WORKER CELEBRATIONS

As I should have made clear earlier, the people who work for us are not called employees—we refer to them as Co-workers. Remember, the first people to work for me were my friends and neighbors. Nobody thought of me as a boss. Nobody had a title, or, for that matter, a specific job. Everyone just did what had to be done. We were a close-knit group and everyone was treated like family—nobody bothered to ring the doorbell. They just walked right in.

Organizing inventory and packing boxes tend to be monotonous. So to add some excitement to otherwise tedious work, we looked for occasions to have fun. To make our work more interesting, we'd celebrate any occasion worth celebrating: someone's birthday, achieving a sales projection. Sometimes we celebrated because we were working so hard and needed to take a break and let off a little steam. Other times, when something went haywire, we'd order a pizza and sit around the table to discuss what we had to do differently. These were great opportunities for us to pull people together.

In the beginning, these celebrations involved only a handful of people—three or four of us, or five or ten of us. Later the numbers started to increase as the business expanded. We finally reached a point when we had so many Co-workers that, had this tradition continued, we'd be celebrating every day of the week. So we decided to hold one celebration a month for everyone who had a birthday or anniversary during the past thirty days. This tradition continued even when we had several different locations, and I attended all of them. Logistically, it could be quite a chore. When we moved everything under one roof in 2002, we were able to accommodate everyone with one big Co-worker celebration, each shift, every month. It's held in a large open space in our distribution center. Everyone in the building attends with the exception of the people on the phone lines, and in those departments Co-workers take turns going.

The premise of today's Co-worker Celebrations remains the same as when a few of us sat around our dining room table eating pizza. We still congratulate everyone with a birthday, service anniversary, or promotion. Now, however, the names are read as all honorees stand together, and one round of applause is given to the entire group. There is plenty of applause; some departments prepare special cheers for their colleagues. A Pampered Chef product is given to each honoree as a token gift, in a shopping bag with the company logo. On occasion, I emcee the event, but usually one of our executives serves as the master of ceremonies. The thirty-to-forty-five minute meeting serves as a platform to make important announcements and recognize people for their achievements. Subjects cover the gamut, including new products, company benefits, or the latest news on our charitable giving programs. Announcements of coming events are also made. Videos run in the backgrounds that feature our conferences, product demonstrations, and recent media coverage about the company. The celebrations help to create a sense of togetherness, a feeling of family in the workplace, because everyone gets together, regardless of position. People who run forklifts sit next to executives or to people who work in the test kitchens. It is a unifying experience. Cookies, doughnuts, and fruit are served, and at the end everyone receives a copy of the latest edition of our company newspaper.

Similar to our monthly Co-worker Celebrations is Appreciation Day, a once-a-year event. This special day is held during the month of September, when everyone is back from summer vacation. On this occasion, we sponsor a lunch or dinner for our Co-workers, to express our appreciation for the hard work put in by everyone for our annual National Conference. While several home-office Co-workers appear on stage during the Conference and receive rounds of applause, there are many more people in support roles who are not recognized. This is our time to recognize our unsung heroes.

YOU MAKE A DIFFERENCE

Another program we've designed to recognize Co-workers is You Make a Difference (YMAD), in which points are awarded to Co-workers who do something above and beyond the normal call of duty. Co-workers earn points in a variety of ways. One category is volunteerism, which includes doing volunteer work for a company event such as assisting at the Conference, a commitment that could involve several long days. Points can also be earned by volunteering in the community at such places as homeless shelters, schools, or food banks, or doing fund-raising for a civic or charitable cause. Co-workers can also earn points for acquiring a new job-related skill, or for submitting suggestions that save time or money for the company or improve our safety practices.

Each quarter, YMAD points can be redeemed for a selection of items that bear the Pampered Chef logo, including mugs, shirts, caps, insulated lunch bags, coolers, and duffel bags. At the highest point levels, we offer a complete set of barbeque tools or a set of Simple Additions ceramic serving pieces.

A committee of Co-workers manages the YMAD program and is responsible for establishing the criteria, selecting the awards, and promoting awareness of the program. Co-workers who have received YMAD points during the previous month are often asked to stand as a group to receive recognition at monthly celebrations. These acknowledgments evoke rounds of applause. The program is important for us in reinforcing our values, recognizing achievement, and building company morale.

AN ONGOING TEAM EFFORT

As someone who has spent many years conducting Kitchen Shows as well as recruiting and training new Consultants, I know the thrill and joy that accompanies a successful Kitchen Show. I also know the frustration that accompanies a poorly attended one. I can feel empathy for a Director who had high hopes for a promising new Consultant who throws in the towel after a disappointing show. Most important, I know how much our people in the field depend on support from the home office. While many CEOs throughout corporate America claim they support their sales organization, few have actually been there. I've been there.

When we at The Pampered Chef say we are a customer-driven company, we mean it. Catering to our sales organization starts at the top—with me, the CEO—and permeates our organization. Our sales organization drives our business—our Kitchen Consultants are our first line to the customer. They are the ones out there with customers every day of the week. At the home office, we recognize that without the sales organization, our jobs wouldn't exist. Knowing this, *everyone's* job is to serve the sales organization. Our Kitchen Consultants are revered and respected. At the same time, our sales organization realizes that to succeed, it is dependent on home-office support. This means that each exists for the benefit of the other. As the CEO of The Pampered Chef, my most important job is to assure an ongoing, harmonious team effort.

By far the biggest event of the year at The Pampered Chef is our National Conference, held at McCormick Place Convention

Center in Chicago. Three to four thousand Kitchen Consultants attend each of these three consecutive Conferences each July. Tens of thousands of hours are put into creating these extravaganzas by our home-office staff. The people at our distribution center package materials to be sent to McCormick Place, working tirelessly to make sure the Conference is a huge success. I've long maintained that our home-office people should be exposed to our Conferences in order to better understand our business. This is why we encourage everyone in our home office to experience our National Conference. Several weeks beforehand, we request them to fill out forms listing the date they would like to attend. Their attendance takes place on company time, and to make getting there convenient, we bus them to the convention center. We want them to be part of the audience, sitting there side by side with our Consultants, sharing the excitement. The more our home-office people understand the sales organization, the better they can support them.

It's a two-way street. We also bring our people from the field to the home office to see what our internal people do. Here, they see firsthand how orders are processed, picked, and packed. This gives them a better understanding about what is being done to service their business.

Our management team is constantly meeting with our top Directors, listening to ideas from the field, searching for ways the home office can give better support. This feedback is a major source of ideas for our new products, including improving existing products. We also have local field directors working with our Directors and their Consultants. These local field directors are served by our Sales Managers. "Since I started in 1995, I've traveled to all fifty states to meet with our Consultants and Directors," says Sales Manager Susie Lite. "I believe direct communication with our sales organization is essential, and nothing beats being there."

When I hired Kathy Kari in 1993, I said to her she would be one of our first full-time home economists, with the title of Product Development Manager. "Although I'm looking for someone in the home office," I told her, "I also want you to be out in the field seeing what's going on. I want you to be hands-on so you will really know what we're all about."

"In my job today as the company's Director of Test Kitchens," Kathy says, "I learned valuable experience in the field that provided me with a clearer understanding of the needs of both the Consultant and the customer. There are now eighteen people in our department, and all of them keep an eye on what's going on at the Kitchen Show. We practice what we preach.

"We're responsible for recipe development. By knowing the intricacies of a Kitchen Show, I have a deeper appreciation for what works in the field. We want a demonstrable recipe that can be done start to finish at the Kitchen Show. This means it should take no more than thirty minutes. And besides being quick, it must be attractive *and* easy. There's also a certain price point so it doesn't cost a ton of money for the host.

"We've also introduced some consumable products to our line," Kathy continues, "such as baking mixes and spice blends. These products offer an opportunity for a Consultant to call back a customer and ask, 'How did your family enjoy the pizza crust and roll mix you bought in January?' By spending time in the field, I learned all sorts of ways I can better serve our Consultants."

DEFINING "IS"

Most companies refer to their technology department as an IT department, short for Information Technology. To others, it's IS, for Information Systems. At The Pampered Chef, we call it Information *Services*—with the emphasis on services. That's because we use technology to provide service.

In our early years, our use of technology was limited to the telephone and an electric typewriter. We did everything manually. Nineteen-eighty was still the era of mainframe computers. Microsoft, founded in 1975 by Bill Gates and Paul Allen, was still in its infancy, and Apple had only moved out of Steve Jobs's garage in 1977. We were as low-tech as a company could be—but then we were on an equal footing with most other start-ups. Times have sure changed. Today, one of the first expenses for the vast majority of start-up companies is the purchase of a computer.

Jay had worked for a company that used technology, and he understood the way it simplified a lot of a company's administrative functions, such as creating financial statements and inventory controls.

At the onset of our recruiting freeze in 1990, we realized that we had to make better use of technology to keep our operations side ahead of our sales revenues. As Linda Stupar, our Director of Order Processing, whom you met earlier, says, "When I first started, the company was processing orders manually. I worked with Jay to find an outside programming company to automate what had been done manually. One of our biggest challenges was converting noncomputer Co-workers to a faster and more accurate way to work. I sat down with each of them individually to convince everyone that what we were doing was the wave of the future. 'Don't think of it as taking away your job. It will assure your job security,' I emphasized."

Prior to Linda's arrival, Jay had been responsible for the nightly closes, month-end procedures, and commissioning entries. Now, Jay delegated these responsibilities to Linda. "Our goal is never to miss a commission run," Jay told her. "You are never to go beyond the eighth of the month. If you do, the field will panic because they'll think the company can't keep up with the growth. So you must get them out on time." Because a high percentage of our orders come in at the end of the month, this can be a real challenge, especially, during the holiday season.

"I still shudder when I think about the time the electricity went out at two a.m. on February 7," Linda recalls. "I was wondering if I was going to have a job if I didn't get those checks out on time. Fortunately, the electricity came back on, and with everyone working overtime, we made our deadline.

"During another holiday season, the one in 1991, the orders were coming in so heavy that I had to hide them in a conference room so the staff wouldn't be overwhelmed. My biggest fear was that they would look at the volume and walk out the door, saying, 'This is impossible.' I had to bring the orders out gradually, so they wouldn't go home crying."

In the beginning, the company's IS department focused on the finance end of our business. Linda directs her staff to process all incoming orders from customers and Consultants, commissionable and noncommissionable (noncommissionable orders are requests for supplies and business materials that the sales organization acquires from the company).

As sales volume skyrocketed, we realized that we had to update our warehousing to get merchandise out the door in a timely fashion. We could no longer use grocery carts to do the job. So we called on our IS people to set up systems in warehousing to assure quality control and the rapid flow of product from the storage bins to the UPS trucks. Today, this is done by a state-of-the-art computerized system that does everything from picking orders to scanning packages to ensure every package contains the right merchandise before it is picked up for delivery. Fulfillment is one of the most important issues within a direct-sales company.

It is in the area of communication between the field and the home office that IS has been an absolute godsend. There was a time when all orders submitted by Consultants were sent by mail. Now 90 percent of our orders are e-mailed to the home office. At first, the sales organization resisted the changeover. Today, the opposite is true. Nonetheless, 10 percent of our orders continue to be processed manually—we don't want to leave out any of our Consultants who lack computer skills.

"We didn't want to jam it down anyone's throat," explains Rich Schubkegel, Information Services Vice President. "When we started electronic ordering in 1995, it wasn't via the Internet—orders were sent by electronic transmission, a modem-to-modem transfer. The first year, less than twenty percent of the field was sending in their orders that way. But each year the percentage kept growing. Information Services actually made it possible to process many more orders with fewer people and fewer errors. We're careful to build systems capable of handling the large number of orders that come in during the last week of the month. I've seen other companies that install systems that can handle their normal flow of business but fail to do the job at their peak times. Consequently, these companies are flooded in back orders that bury them."

"A majority of the orders come in via Pampered Partner, our proprietary software program," continues Schubkegel. "A Consultant keys in an order and it automatically balances her order, so when it's received, there are no mistakes. At this point, the only thing we have to do is check for credit card authorization."

When Consultants have a problem with Pampered Partner software or our Web site, they can call our toll-free number for technical support. Often, however, a new Consultant will first seek help from the person in her cluster who recruited her. We also have a user manual and videotapes on how to use the different software. And of course, we offer workshops that Consultants can attend at the Conference and other times during the year.

Now, since the advent of the Internet, a Director can go online anytime to get current production figures on the Consultants in her cluster. In the past, these numbers were available only at the end of the month. Today many of our Consultants have their own personal Web sites that they use for such things as sending out electronic invitations to Kitchen Shows, reconfirming bookings, and taking outside orders. With an abundance of technology to support our sales organization, we work overtime to avoid becoming impersonal. We don't want to be one of those companies where you never talk to a person, you just keep talking to machines until you get disconnected. To avoid this, we're constantly monitoring calls at our call centers, and reviewing issues ranging from caller satisfaction to an acceptable hold time. In today's world, we couldn't function without technology.

According to Ralph Van Dyke, our computer operations manager, everything in our company today runs through IS. Ralph's number one responsibility is to make sure the systems never fail. "We work in a heterogeneous environment," he says, "with all types of platforms, operating systems, PCs, switchers, routers, hubs, voice systems, and servers. There is always a crisis brewing—always. At this very moment there are probably two or three going on. The beauty of it is, we always fix it. We have the staff and we've been allowed to obtain the tools. We've been given the freedom to effectively manage our environment."

Nevertheless, despite all the technology we have in place today to make everything easy for our Consultants, we are first and foremost a people company. We use our technology to serve our people. When properly executed, technology is a tool to make things easier for our people, to help make them more efficient. When a customer sees a product that she likes at our Web site, all she has to do is click on "To Purchase Product" and she's linked to one of our Kitchen Consultants. And that makes buying our merchandise easy for customers and Consultants.

THE JOY OF GIVING

While considerable change has occurred since the company was founded, the one thing that has remained constant is our mission to help families come together around the dinner table. From my first Kitchen Show, I have enjoyed teaching women how to use kitchen tools, knowing that it would translate into happier families. From the beginning, my focus has been not on how much money I would make, but on how others would benefit. I have always believed that doing good for others is also good business. Jay and I have strong feelings about giving back. As the Bible says, "to whom much has been given, much will be required." We have been blessed with much and feel privileged to give back to our community and our country. We feel this is our responsibility, and one that we do not take lightly.

As a company, we've put a lot of thought into our charitable giving. After much deliberation, we decided to support three major causes. Each is related to women and the family. First, to help all families to put meals on the table, The Pampered Chef has become a major supporter of America's Second Harvest, the nation's largest network of food banks that supply to food pantries, soup kitchens, churches, and other food relief organizations across the country. Second, we sponsor a program at the University of Illinois in Urbana-Champaign to study issues of family resiliency and explore what behaviors strengthen family bonds. We believe The Pampered Chef Family Resiliency Program will make significant strides in helping families to become stronger and more resilient in the face of today's challenges. And third, we created a campaign called Help Whip Cancer, in conjunction with the American Cancer Society, to provide funds for the education about and early detection of breast cancer.

We constantly invite our Consultants and Co-workers to join us in making a difference. For instance, in a campaign called Round-Up from the Heart, we encourage our Consultants to have their customers round up their orders to the nearest dollar or more. A $24.55 order, for example, could be rounded up to $25; the extra 45 cents goes to an America's Second Harvest local food bank. Customers also can purchase commemorative products sold specifically to raise funds through the Round-Up from the Heart campaign. A donation is made for each commemorative product purchased. These funds are sent to America's Second Harvest's headquarters in Chicago, where the money is used to buy food in bulk for food banks throughout the country. Every penny contributed is used to help end hunger in America.

Although the amounts are only pennies here and there, at the end of the year, these contributions are significant. Over the years, these pennies, nickels, dimes, and quarters have added up to millions of dollars to feed the hungry. I am so grateful and proud of our Consultants and our customers who support this worthy cause.

To promote family resiliency, The Pampered Chef made a

five-year financial commitment in 2000 to the University of Illinois to sponsor faculty research grants and graduate fellowships to strengthen families. This program also invites renowned scholars to speak on family resiliency. The lectures range from what makes families strong to why some families are more capable than others of surviving hardships. The Pampered Chef has also endowed a chair in family resiliency at the university. Recently we've extended our commitment to the university through the year 2009. Our dedication to building strong families goes beyond family mealtimes.

Through our Help Whip Cancer program, we have joined forces with the American Cancer Society to promote the importance of early breast cancer detection. During the entire month of May each year, our Consultants raise funds from the sale of limited-edition products and special Help Whip Cancer Kitchen Show fund-raisers. At these Kitchen Shows, our Consultants tell customers about the importance of regular breast cancer screening and checkups; after all, the five-year survival rate for women diagnosed at an early stage is more than 97 percent. The funds we collect are distributed to promote breast cancer education and early detection programs across the United States.

We honor our Consultants who have been the most active in the Round-Up from the Heart and Help Whip Cancer campaigns at our National Conference by inviting them to an event called "the Breakfast of Caring." About one thousand Consultants attend this breakfast at each of our three Conferences.

The Pampered Chef Kitchen Consultants continue to host special fund-raising Kitchen Shows. At such shows, a percentage of all sales under $600 goes to the charity of the host's choice, and a higher percentage is donated for sales over $600. It's a win-win for everyone.

We also have two food drives at our headquarters each year:

National Hunger Awareness Day, during the first week in June; and the entire month of November. Our Co-workers distribute food we collect to the Northern Illinois Food Bank in St. Charles, our area's local food bank. Every fall we also offer volunteering opportunities at our local food bank, for which we provide transportation, snacks, and beverages. As an incentive to our Co-workers for volunteering in the community, YMAD points are awarded.

In addition, each year, our Bright Futures Scholarship Program awards educational scholarships to twenty children of Consultants and ten children of Co-workers.

Giving back is important in everything we do. That is why when The Pampered Chef joined Berkshire Hathaway on October 31, 2002, Jay and I presented every Co-worker with a $1,000 bonus for each year he or she had worked for the company. I had the honor of personally presenting checks to each Co-worker with ten or more years of service with the company. This was our way of saying, "Thank you. You made a difference."

HAVING A SUCCESSION PLAN

Some business leaders make no plans for their untimely demise, sudden disability, or retirement. Sometimes, it's a matter of neglect—it's something they intend to get around to but simply don't. Other times, these individuals think they are indispensable and irreplaceable. Their egos get in the way. But not having a succession plan, in my opinion, is simply bad business.

A business leader has a responsibility to her stockholders, employees, vendors, and customers to assure them that their future is intact. This is what a succession plan does. It provides a prearranged way for an organization to effect a seamless transition in the event of a change of leadership. Employees know the company will continue to operate and their jobs will be secure. Vendors know that their products will continue to be needed. Customers know they will continue to have a source to obtain needed products and services.

The U.S. Army places such importance on succession plans that it requires every officer to have multiple subordinates ready to take over his or her job. General Electric has an "emergency leader-in-waiting," should something happen to its CEO. The principle is simple: the fate of the organization is more important than the fate of its leader. A qualified person must be able to step in in the event of a catastrophe so that business can continue as usual.

Over the years, Jay and I have seen a lot of good people hurt because they worked for, or did business with, a company that did not have a succession plan in place. Concerned for our Consultants, Co-workers, and vendors, we decided that we needed a succession plan, and that time to install one was *now*. Succession planning was what ultimately led us to Warren Buffett. We decided to take action before we had to, believing that when you have to, it's too late. I was in good health, there was no financial reason to do it—we didn't need the money. We did it because we felt we had a responsibility to fulfill. We wanted the people in our sales organization and home-office people to be assured that our business was secure beyond the time that I would be here to run it. We wanted to pick the time to make this transfer rather than being forced to do it by external pressure.

We thought about a public offering and met with some Wall Street investment bankers, such as Goldman Sachs. One of Goldman Sachs's contacts was Berkshire Hathaway's Warren Buffett, whom Jay and I have long admired. When we talked about the kind of company that we'd like to be associated with, Berkshire Hathaway was an ideal candidate. It's a company with high stakes in prestigious companies such as American Express and Coca-Cola, and a company that didn't interfere with the way its affiliated companies were operated by their managers. So I went to Omaha to meet with Mr. Buffett. What interested him the most was: (1) our revenues had grown by 232 percent from 1995 to 2001, compared with the industry's 49 percent gain; (2) other than the $3,000 that we borrowed on Jay's life insurance policy, the company had never had any debt; (3) our pretax margins were healthy; and (4) we had vast potential for growth compared to other companies in our industry. After making an offer, Mr. Buffett attended an Omaha Kitchen Show where he participated in an apple-peeling contest. And the rest is history. Within three weeks we signed a contract, and in October of 2002, The Pampered Chef became a proud member of the Berkshire Hathaway family.

It is a wonderful compliment that Warren Buffett, arguably the nation's most astute judge of businesses, recognized the value in our company. True to our expectations regarding Mr. Buffett's style of management, he has never interfered with the running of The Pampered Chef. This, I believe, is a tribute to his amazing success as a businessperson and investor.

With today's seasoned, professional management team, I feel certain we have a strong succession plan in place.

8

THE WORLD'S GREATEST SALES ORGANIZATION

Nobody knows better than I how much our sales organization contributes to our success. As someone once said, "Nothing happens until something is sold." Without our sales organization, the company would not exist. It is by far our most valuable asset.

While we've had enormous change and growth over the past twenty-five years, the Kitchen Show remains the centerpiece of our business. This is why we will always put our sales organization first. It is the heart and soul of our business. Everything we do at The Pampered Chef revolves around the Kitchen Show.

While I speak about our sales organization collectively, it is a diverse group of people who live in countless places throughout the United States, Canada, and the United Kingdom. They come from many different backgrounds, representing a wide array of ethnic groups, ages, education, and work experience. During the past twenty-five years, I have met thousands of them; each has an interesting personal story. It is not possible to tell you about each of them individually, but I want to relate ten success stories that I think are representative of the people in our sales organization.

Selecting ten out of so many thousands of successful people was my most challenging task in writing this book. I feel like a proud mother who wants to show off her beautiful children, but can carry only so many photos in her wallet. Believe me, there are so many of our Consultants I can rave about; it would take volumes to tell you about all of them. With this in mind, remember that the ten people I've singled out here represent many, many thousands of others.

SCOTTIE BRISTER

Scottie Brister, who had been a schoolteacher, joined the company in June 2001. She has received numerous awards for top performance in personal sales and recruiting. Scottie, her husband Shane, and their two children live in Louisiana.

"In October 2000 I was invited to a Pampered Chef show ten miles north of here," Scottie says. "I had never heard of the company. 'Just come hungry,' I was told. Well, I knew I could do that, so I promised I'd be there.

"At the Kitchen Show, I was overwhelmed by the kitchen products. Later, when Vicki Mahan, the Kitchen Consultant, passed out company literature and order forms, she told me, 'Just circle all the things you like.' Well, circles are free! I got so excited, I just circled all kinds of stuff. But when it came time to pay for everything, I told her I couldn't afford everything.

" 'Why don't you host a party?' Vicki suggested. 'This way you'll get some free products.' "

A month later, Scottie hosted a Kitchen Show, still talked

about as "the show of shows of the South." Known to her family and friends as an organizer—she plans everything from reunions to parties—Scottie invited thirty people to her house for the Kitchen Show: co-workers, friends, and family members. Fellow teachers who were unable to attend were given a Pampered Chef catalog. When Vicki Mahan came to the Brister house that night to conduct the show, Scottie handed her $800 worth of presold orders even before the first guest arrived! The Show generated another $1,000 in sales.

"Vicki was just flipping out," Scottie says. "Later she told me that when she got in her car, she immediately called her husband. 'Get out a calculator,' she told him, and rattled off the orders she had taken to see how much they totaled."

With bonuses, Scottie ended up with $500 worth of free products. "I was like a kid in a candy store, hardly knowing what to order first. It was like shopping and getting everything for free," she recalls. "I still wanted more things, so I planned to host another show. I kept a catalog on the side of my refrigerator of the stuff I wanted to get. Meanwhile, Vicki kept in touch, encouraging me to become a Consultant.

"I kept telling her I wasn't interested. But Vicki continued to send me flyers with my consent. The following June at the end of the school year, thinking about all the free products I could get, I signed up to be a Consultant. My plan was to pay the hundred dollars for the kit—which came with a few hundred dollars' worth of products; if I did six shows by July 5, I'd earn additional merchandise as a bonus. That was my goal, to load my kitchen with Pampered Chef products, and make a little extra spending money on the side.

"At the time, I had only one child, although I was six and a half months pregnant. School was out so I got on the phone and started calling people.

" 'Will you host a Kitchen Show for me?' I asked the people

I called. When they agreed, I said, 'Great, but it has to be by the fifth of July'—so I could earn a free muffin stone. 'Okay, I'll put you down for a week from next Tuesday.' In a day or so, I had all six shows booked.

"So I called Vicki. 'This is Scottie, remember me? Okay, I've got six shows booked. I need a kit so I can get started. My first show is only ten days away.' Vicki was so excited, she rushed right over, had me fill out some forms, and gave me packets for my two sisters and friends who had also booked shows so they could start inviting people. Vicki had a show coming up that week, so I went with her to learn how to give one, taking notes. One woman at the show, a friend of my mom's, asked, 'Are you signing up, Scottie? I'd love to do a show for you.'

"My first show was at my best friend's home. My second was at my sister Stephanie's. My middle sister was there and told me, 'Oh, I know you're not going to stay with it, so I am going to book a show in December.' So I told her I was going to hold her to it. My first show's sales totaled $421 and I made $84. It practically covered the entire cost of my kit. My second show grossed $394, so I made my kit money back plus a little more. By the time I had done six shows, I had fifteen bookings. I sold $2,700 in my first month and $5,554 in my second month. I did nine shows that second month, including two thousand-dollar shows, as well as setting up twenty bookings! My second commission check was just five hundred dollars short of what I made teaching full time. And I made that money in a lot less time than the hours I put into work at school, and I had a lot more fun."

Scottie, a certified physical education teacher, taught kindergarten through fourth grade. A former volleyball player who had earned a full athletic scholarship at Southeastern Louisiana, she returned to her hometown to teach at the local elementary school. Four years later she became the coach of girls' track and basketball, realizing a longtime ambition. But the coaching job demanded long hours, and with the birth of her second child she was unhappy that her work required her to be away from home so much of the time. Because of that, during the school year, she didn't devote much time to her Pampered Chef career, doing only the occasional Kitchen Show to keep active. But when summer came, Scottie became active again, booking more shows. In June 2003, her sales totaled $6,000. Vicki, her Director, called to say, "Congratulations! You went over five thousand dollars for the month and you've brought in a recruit. If you do five thousand a month and sign up one recruit a month for three consecutive months, you'll be invited to Heritage Table."

"That's for the big dogs," Scottie replied. "I'm only in this for the fun. When school starts, I'll be back teaching again."

A few weeks later Cora Fischer called from the home office to congratulate her, telling her that she was on track to be invited to Heritage Table. "There will be fifteen from the Southern region attending Heritage Home, the Christophers' home where the business first started. You'll get to meet Doris and Jay."

"I felt so honored to receive that call," Scottie remembers. "It gave me added incentive to work hard to become one of those fifteen consultants from the region. And I did it. I was thrilled—I'd accomplished something I didn't think I could do. At the meeting, they called out everyone's names to recognize the top performers, starting with the person who was fifteenth, fourteenth, and so on. I kept waiting for my name, but it wasn't called. Finally they announced the final three and I was third out of all the Consultants from the South. I could hardly believe it. Diane Engle, my National Senior Executive Director from Louisiana, congratulated me. I was on cloud nine."

During her visit to Heritage Home, Scottie talked with the other top performers, who encouraged her to pursue a Pampered

Chef career full time. She was convinced. "When I came home, I told Shane my plans.

" 'I know you've been really stressed out teaching,' he said. 'And you have more passion for this work than your school job. Hannah is four, and Ethan is going on two; doing Pampered Chef full time will give you more flexibility to schedule your work around them.' He was behind me 100 percent.

"The next day I met with the principal of the high school to tell him my decision. He asked if I'd finish the semester in January. I didn't want to leave him hanging, so I agreed.

"When I told my parents my decision, my father, who is an independent insurance agent, wasn't sure I'd made the right move. 'You went to college to be a teacher and coach,' he said. 'I've told you since you were a little girl that a quitter never wins, and a winner never quits.'

" 'That's right, Daddy,' I answered. 'I've never been known to quit anything, and that hasn't changed. Instead, I'm refocusing. I'm not quitting. Don't you see I'll be teaching people at shows? And I'll be coaching people in my cluster.'

"After I sat down with him and explained what I was doing part time, and that I believed I would succeed at this, he supported my decision. Meanwhile, I qualified for the Pampered Chef Hawaii trip. The following May 2004, my husband and I had the time of our lives in Hawaii! By end of the trip, Shane had met a lot of successful Pampered Chef people and their spouses, and had fallen in love with the company. My dad has also become a huge supporter. It's great having my mom and dad out there spreading the word.

"In my first eight months of doing this full time, I've recruited and built a strong team. I signed up seventeen people in one three-week period. Now I have the added responsibility of making sure they're successful, too. Knowing how I respond to recognition, I'm constantly praising them, encouraging them to go as far as they can in this business. I let them know that I'm always there for them. I just want them all to know that I'm here to help them get whatever they want out of it.

"As far as my own personal goal," Scottie concludes, "I want to see consistent growth in my business, and keep seeing it get better and better. And to one day become a National Senior Executive Director."

TANYA BROSLAWSKY

Tanya Broslawsky is a Senior Director who lives in West Virginia with her husband and two sons. Tanya became a Kitchen Consultant in 1995. She led the company in personal sales production for four consecutive years.

In January 1995, Tanya Broslawsky reluctantly attended a Kitchen Show hosted by her next-door neighbor. "I did it as a favor," she explains. "I didn't do much cooking, and I wasn't into home parties, so I really had little interest. My neighbor said to me, 'You won't have to buy anything, Tanya. Just come. I need you as a warm body.'

"I went with my guard up, but to my surprise, it was fun," Tanya says. "I was surprised at how laid back it was—there was absolutely no pressure to buy anything. I learned a little about cooking, and I was impressed to see high-quality cookware that didn't stick. I didn't want to pay full price, so I volunteered to host a show."

Tanya was a full-time nurse at University Hospital in Morgantown, West Virginia, about forty miles north of her hometown, working the weekend midnight shift—twelve hours every

Friday, Saturday, and Sunday. Her commute took her over mountainous, twisting West Virginia roads, one hour each way; the long trip home after a grueling night at the hospital was especially tiresome. Her husband Jim, a schoolteacher, worked Monday through Friday, so Tanya and Jim took turns spending time with their two young sons. But the Broslawskys were rarely able to do things together as a family.

"It's a hard way to live," Tanya explains. "But you make sacrifices for your children. When I went to nursing school I knew I might end up working nights. I love nursing and I was willing to do whatever the job required, but I didn't like being away from my family.

"One early morning around five a.m., I was talking to another nurse. About that time of morning you start considering other occupations. 'There must be another job that doesn't demand these hours,' my girlfriend said to me. And I told her about the Pampered Chef show I hosted in January. I told her, 'If money can be made this way, why don't we try it?' At first we both laughed about it, but a few conversations later, we got serious. That July, nearly seven months after hosting my first show, I talked to Jim about becoming a Kitchen Consultant.

"Jim's reaction was, 'If you want to make some extra money, then do it.' "

During her first few months with the company, Tanya did two to three shows a month and recruited her girlfriend, the nurse she worked with at the hospital. "I had no intention of quitting my nursing job," she explains. "I didn't want to become a full-time Kitchen Consultant. I just wanted the diversion of doing something far removed from my work at the hospital. Yes, it provided a little extra money, but at the time I was content with what I made at the hospital.

"I suppose what made working that midnight shift on weekends tolerable," Tanya continues, "was the extra six-fifty an hour we received to work it. But then the hospital hired a new director of nursing who thought we were overpaid, so she took that shift differential away from us. Suddenly, working that midnight shift became less tolerable.

"At this point, I began to reevaluate my nursing career and my lifestyle. My love for nursing didn't make up for being away from my family on weekends and holidays. Jim didn't work from June through August, and we would have loved to take extended summer vacations like other teachers' families did, but with my job we couldn't. And each Kitchen Show made me realize how much I loved this work. I thrive on helping people, and while I wasn't saving lives, I was performing a valuable service, teaching them how to cook easily, quickly—and with the best kitchen tools on the market. I liked the fact that I was helping them to improve their lives. Like nursing, it was very rewarding."

Prior to joining The Pampered Chef, Tanya didn't enjoy cooking. "I'd make the basic stuff like casseroles, but being in the kitchen wasn't my thing," she confesses. "It's probably because my mother taught high school home economics; she would get up at five-thirty every morning, making everything from scratch. It was a real ordeal, and then my dad and four brothers wolfed it down in fifteen minutes. 'What a waste of time!' I thought. I never wanted to dedicate so much time to preparing meals. Today, however, I love making different recipes for my family and I love it when someone calls to say, 'Thank you so much for teaching me how to make that dish. I cooked it last night and my husband loved it!' "

Four years after Tanya signed up for her first Kitchen Show, she decided to leave her job at the hospital to work full time as a Pampered Chef consultant. "I quit my nursing job on August 3, 1999," she says, grinning. "I know the exact date because that was my last clock-out."

Tanya brought the same work ethic she exercised as a nurse to her Pampered Chef career. Gone were the long twelve-hour days on weekends with the daily two-hour round-trip commute, but with her passion for her new line of work, Tanya averaged twenty Kitchen Shows a month and her sales soared. For four consecutive years, she was our company's top seller. "My husband likes to joke that my wife only does shows on days that end with the letter Y."

More recently, Tanya has focused her energies on building a strong cluster of Consultants working under her. She currently has 120 people in her cluster, and growing. Today she has her sights set on becoming a National Senior Executive Director, and with her determination and savvy I think she'll achieve it. "The support we get from the home office is endless," she says. "There isn't any reason not to succeed. We all start out with the same kit, so it's a matter of what we do with the opportunity we're given."

"I realized that at the hospital I received recognition only rarely," she says. "Getting so much recognition now makes me realize how much I needed it. I loved the free products to reward my sales delivered to my doorstep, the all-expenses-paid Pampered Chef trips. This past year I took my son to Hawaii as my high school graduation present to him. One reason workers' morale is so low in corporate America is because management doesn't give them enough recognition. Everyone needs to be praised. I *know* this for a fact because I know how much it drives me."

How is she able to sell so much in her small West Virginia town with a population of only eight thousand? "I don't limit my territory," she explains. "I work the entire area in Bridgeport, Clarksburg, Fairmont, and Morgantown; I go into nearby Pennsylvania and Maryland. I'll drive two hours away to give a show. The company ships everything UPS to the hostess, so it doesn't really matter where I give a show. For example, while I was visiting a friend in Connecticut, I did a few shows, and now I'm in the process of building a team up there. I go there periodically to conduct training sessions."

Tanya claims that living and working in a small town has been a big advantage. She appreciates the small-town values of the people in her surrounding area. "They don't eat out nearly as much," she points out, "and because they don't have the long commutes back and forth to work like people in large metropolitan areas, they come home earlier, which gives them more time to spend in the kitchen."

Tanya's advice to women is: "Don't be afraid to do something outside your comfort zone. Be tenacious! You can do anything you want in life, if you want it badly enough.

"In my former life at the hospital, I looked forward to retirement because I was so unhappy with my job. Looking back, what a terrible thing it is to wish your life away! Today, I no longer think about retirement because I'm making a difference in people's lives and I'm having fun doing it."

GIL CHARLEBOIS

Gil Charlebois lives in Ontario, Canada, in a town of eighty people seventy miles north of Toronto. When he joined The Pampered Chef in September 1997, Gil was working full time as a mail carrier at the post office. He is currently a Director and has twenty people in his cluster.

Knowing her husband's passion for cooking, when Helene Charlebois attended a Pampered Chef Kitchen Show, she couldn't wait to tell her husband what she'd bought.

"What do you think?" she asked when she described her purchases to him.

"They're wonderful," he said excitedly. "How come you didn't buy more?"

"I decided to host a show," she answered, telling him what that meant.

Gil was more excited than his wife about her hosting a show. But when the first guests arrived, Helene asked Gil to stay downstairs in the playroom to watch their four small children. "I don't want the children upstairs making a lot of noise," Helene said. "I need you to babysit them."

Gil managed to quiet down the children. When the show started, he tiptoed upstairs and took a seat in the back of the room to observe. He was fascinated by what he saw.

After the show ended and only the Consultant remained, Gil told his wife, "This is a wonderful opportunity. I never knew it existed."

"Yes," the Consultant replied, "and I think Helene will be good at it."

"I was thinking it's something I would like to do," Gil answered sheepishly.

"You?"

"Why not?" he asked. "I'm the one who does most of the cooking in our house. It's what I love to do."

"Well, I don't know of any men who do this, but I don't suppose there is a reason why you can't."

Gil's comment caught the Consultant off guard. For one thing, Gil was more of an introvert, and seemed a most unlikely candidate to be The Pampered Chef's first male Kitchen Consultant in Canada.

"I developed arthritis at age thirty," Gil says. "At the time I was doing manual labor that involved heavy lifting, and I had to give that up to take a job at the post office. I was looking for something else. With my love for cooking I thought I'd try this on a part-time basis. I figured I'd give ten shows, get some Pampered Chef products I wanted, and that would be the end of it. I had never sold a thing in my life; I had no idea I would enjoy selling so much!"

Helene accompanied her husband to all his shows for the next eighteen months. "In the beginning, I felt uncomfortable going to a woman's house because I was concerned about what a husband might think," Gil explains. "I also needed my wife to be with me for moral support. I was quite shy and speaking to a group of women was really nerve-racking. It was also helpful to have Helene there to help set things up, fill out order forms, and so on.

"We were fortunate to have a babysitter for our four children who charged us five dollars for the entire night, and she preferred that we give her Pampered Chef products rather than money. Eventually, Helene got tired of coming to shows; by then, I had gotten over my shyness and no longer felt I needed her as my security blanket. It's interesting how much this work has changed my personality. I discovered I thrive on being in front of a group of people, and giving Kitchen Shows.

"There was a time when my arthritis was quite bad. Although it never prevented me from cooking or giving shows, I had difficulty gripping and lifting something heavy." Gil pauses for a moment. "It probably seems strange to say this, but I think enjoying what I'm doing has helped to ease my arthritic pain. I figure it probably has something to do with natural endorphins released from doing what I love. Since I was a young lad, I've always enjoyed cooking, and now it's part of my work. Because I'm good at it, I receive many compliments. This never happened with any other job I've ever had."

Three years later, at age forty-two, Gil decided to leave his full-time job at the post office to become a full-time Kitchen Consultant. He admits it took courage to give up the security of a steady paycheck every week, but he feels it was well worth it. To-day, his earnings are considerably greater than what he had made at the post office. "Besides, the stress level at the post office was very high," he says. "In comparison, this is truly stress-free."

Gil says that the best fringe benefit is the travel awards he has earned. "We could never afford a luxury vacation," he explains, "and now we've been to places like Cancun and Maui. Our first Pampered Chef trip was to Hawaii, and airfare alone for one person was fifteen hundred dollars. The funny thing is, after I qual-ified for the trip, I told Helene, 'I'm not sure I want to go.'

" 'Why not?' she asked.

" 'Well, it's probably going to be "Rah, rah, Pampered Chef!" all the time, and you know I wouldn't like that.'

" 'Come on,' she said, 'we'll go and enjoy it.'

"In our twelve years of marriage, we had never taken a trip, so we decided to go. When we got there, the first day The Pam-pered Chef had a luau to welcome us. Doris stood up and greeted everyone. 'I'm so happy to see each of you here. You've all earned it, and that's all I'm going to say about The Pampered Chef. I just want you all to have a wonderful time.' That was it. There was no other official business. The only talk about business was the con-versations we had with our peers. We had a terrific time."

In 2001, to celebrate The Pampered Chef's fifth anniversary in Canada, we held a Conference in Chicago attended by five hundred Canadian Kitchen Consultants. As one of the top Cana-dian Consultants, Gil was a featured speaker. Later he was invited to conduct a workshop at our 2003 Conference in Toronto. "It was amazing," he says. "There I was, a guy who was once so in-troverted that I was afraid to speak to more than two people at a time, and I had absolutely zero nervousness. In fact, I loved it.

"You know, there was a time when I felt sorry for myself be-cause of my arthritis. But if it were not for having arthritis and needing to find other work, I probably would have never come to work for The Pampered Chef. And because I did, I developed self-confidence. To me, my self-esteem is worth all the money in the world. It's something you can't buy."

BARBARA DUKE

Executive Director Barbara Duke lives in northern California. When Barbara joined The Pampered Chef in 1991, she was a full-time paralegal working for a law firm in Sacramento, as well as owning and operating a catering business.

In 1991, The Pampered Chef had a sparse presence in California, consisting mainly of a few scattered consultants who had relocated to the Golden State and continued to sell our products. A few others in California had been recruited when they visited relatives or friends in the Midwest. The rest of our California sales force were women who had signed up when one of our Directors was vacationing on the West Coast. Our Consultants were spread out all over the state, and there was no organized activity. It was no secret that we wanted to establish a stronger foothold in California.

"My daughter Linette, a recent graduate of San Jose State University, attended a Kitchen Show in the Bay Area in the summer of 1990," Barbara says. "For Christmas she bought me a baking stone and a wonder cup, now known as the measure-all cup. I owned my own catering company, and Linette knew I appreciated high-quality kitchen tools. When she told me where she'd gotten them, I asked 'Can you get me one of their catalogs?'

"After going through the catalog, I saw all sorts of things that I wanted to have for my catering business as well as for my own kitchen. I couldn't afford to buy everything, so I called the Consultant in the Bay Area and said I wanted to host a show. She was pregnant and didn't want to drive to Roseville. I had read some literature about the company and I thought, 'I could do this.' I signed up as a Consultant so I could get a kit. I wasn't planning to sell anything. I just wanted to get some Pampered Chef products at a low price. My plan was to get the stuff and quit. But first I had to have a party because I felt it was the right thing to do.

"Since nobody had ever heard of The Pampered Chef, I decided to have the party at my house. Several women said they'd host one if they liked what they saw. 'Just come and see if you like it,' I told them. 'And you can bail on me if you totally hate what you see.'

"I invited everyone I knew to come to my house, telling them how much fun we were going to have: friends, neighbors, co-workers, and wives of the lawyers at the law firm where I worked in Sacramento, which was a forty-minute commute from my house in Roseville. About forty people came, but without any training, I was clueless on what I was supposed to do. They came because I was so excited—that's still what attracts people to our Kitchen Shows."

Barbara's sales for the evening were $800, high for a Kitchen Show in 1991, but low considering forty people attended. "Nobody had instructed me how to fill out the paperwork to process the order," she explains, "and back then we didn't have computers. Without instructions, I was overwhelmed. But I forged through it. We all had such a good time that first night that I booked six shows. I kept getting more bookings and it started snowballing. I've never run out of prospects since."

Barbara continued working at the law firm and running her catering company; she found time to do Kitchen Shows in her free time. "I don't remember how or when it happened," she explains, "but somebody told me that there were Pampered Chef people earning significant income, and when I heard that, I became determined to become one of them. Everyone thought I was nuts. But I suppose I said it enough times that I believed it would happen. I started putting three-by-five cards in green ink on my bathroom mirror, my computer, and my car visor. Well, believe it or not, in my fifth year, I made $150,000. I had only a high school education, so while I was making decent money as a paralegal, I was limited in how far I could go.

"My law firm gave me a token hundred-dollar-a-month raise every year," Barbara continues. "I was a very good paralegal, so I had a lot of job security, which enabled me to negotiate more time off in lieu of a pay raise. As a result, each year I was working fewer hours at the law firm; this allowed me to put in more time at my Pampered Chef business. Just short of four years with The Pampered Chef, I left the law firm. At the time, I was working there only thirty-three hours a week. By then, my Pampered Chef earnings were around six thousand dollars a month, which was a lot more than I made as a paralegal, and even more than the newer attorneys. Today, I make more than some of the firm's partners."

Barbara's rise to success was not exactly a piece of cake. At the time, we had only minor representation on the West Coast, and we didn't have the support system we have today. She also had another handicap. As a result of an abusive childhood, Barbara has spasmodic dysphonia, which she refers to as a voice challenge.

Though Barbara is an attractive and youthful woman, her voice sounds strained. As a result, prior to her Pampered Chef career, Barbara was afraid of public speaking. "Being extremely fearful of speaking," she says, "I wasn't a good candidate for this business. But I was determined to overcome my fear, and I figured the more I spoke, the more I'd get over it.

"Whenever I speak in front of a group, I know people are somewhat taken back because I sound different from what they expect," Barbara says. "When they first hear me, they think I'm really struggling or that it's painful for me to speak. They imagine all kinds of things. So to break the ice at a Kitchen Show, I make a joke up front that lets everyone know I'm comfortable with the way I am, so they feel easier. I might say, 'You probably noticed that my voice is a little unusual. Sometimes when I get tired or really stressed, my voice completely disappears. So, don't be stressing me out tonight or you are going to be up here wearing this apron.' It's part of my routine."

It was the money that first attracted her to the business. "I was so excited about the opportunity that I couldn't imagine why everyone wasn't doing this." With her enthusiasm, she became a Director in November, just seven months after starting her Pampered Chef career. She became, in fact, our first Director in the state of California. Once the company recognized what an asset we had in Barbara, I made several trips to California to work with her and her cluster. I've gotten to know her well over the years, thanks too to our trips together to places like Rome and Hong Kong.

"While it was the money that first motivated me," Barbara says, "I realized that overcoming my personal handicap could serve as an inspiration to other people. Today, this is what drives me. Sure, the commission checks are wonderful, but being in a position to help others believe in themselves is what gives me the most satisfaction."

Barbara was also able to provide an opportunity for her husband to retire. "With my income, Barry could sell his dental laboratory in 1998; today he gets in a lot of golf, which he enjoys so much. And I get so much pleasure out of seeing him enjoying life."

In 2000, Barbara was the recipient of the Pampered Chef Legacy Award, an honor presented to an individual who has influenced our business in a profound and lasting way, in recognition of her pioneering our business in the state of California. At the time she received the award, Barbara had been an Executive

Director for five years and had contributed to the development of 144 Directors in her overall cluster. Today, there are approximately 1,200 people in her cluster.

One of my fondest memories of Barbara dates from the time I came to California to attend a meeting of her cluster, and she organized a potluck dinner. Later in that trip, Barbara and Barry took me to a lovely restaurant. As we dined, Barry Duke said to me, "Thank you so much, Doris, for the opportunity you provided for my wife and me."

"Thank you for all you and Barbara have done for us," I replied, with tears in my eyes.

JULIE GIZZI

Julie Gizzi became a Pampered Chef Consultant in 1996. She is currently a Senior Director, recognized many times by the company for her personal sales and recruiting performance. She and her husband Michael and their son Nicholas live in Colorado.

In 1995 Julie lived in upstate New York, where her husband was attending graduate school. After completing a graduate program at St. Bernard's Institute, a theology school in Rochester, New York, she worked full time in religious education and youth ministry.

"A co-worker invited me to a Kitchen Show," Julie remembers. "I told her, 'I don't go to those things.' I was concerned about the Kitchen Show being too expensive; I had little disposable income. And I didn't want to be subjected to a pushy sales pitch.

"My friend begged me to come, and I finally gave in. 'But I'm not buying anything.' I went to the show and absolutely fell in love with the products. I ended up buying a garlic press; two months later, I hosted my own show. We moved to Colorado, where my husband took a job as a political science professor at Mesa State College. I got a job in youth ministry, similar to the one I had in upstate New York."

Julie quickly discovered that the area's high elevation had an adverse effect on her baking. However, the baking stones that she acquired at the Kitchen Show she hosted back east resolved her problem.

"Not long afterward, I had one of those frustrating days at work where I wanted to pull my hair out," she says. "I was thinking that there had to be something better out there for me. I glanced through the classified ads in our local newspaper and I came across an ad that read 'Love to cook? Start a Pampered Chef business.' I thought, Ah, I love those products. I called the phone number in the ad and talked to Dee Ann Hohn, a Pampered Chef Director who lived a few hours south of me in Colorado.

"I explained to Dee that I had hosted a show in upstate New York, and I told her I was having a difficult time baking out here without stoneware. 'I think I'm interested in this business,' I said. Dee agreed to come up to see me. A few days later, she visited, and I signed up that day.

"I had no intention of quitting my full-time youth ministry work. I only wanted to get the company's stoneware products and make some extra money to buy airfare tickets so we could visit our parents on the East Coast. That was my goal."

At the time, the Gizzis didn't have children and Julie was working sixty hours a week at her full-time job. Even with her long hours, Julie was able to get in some Kitchen Shows. "This was my social outlet," she says. "Plus I could get free kitchen products." Eighteen months later, Julie gave birth to a healthy baby boy, Nicholas.

"Up until this time, I treated The Pampered Chef as more of

a hobby than a real job," Julie says. "Now, Michael and I faced a decision: We could either put Nicholas into day care, which we didn't want to do, or I could become a stay-at-home mom and we'd have to cut back on our standard of living. It was my husband who saw the potential in my 'hobby.' He suggested, 'Why don't you give this everything you've got and quit your full-time job?' That's when we calculated what I'd have to make as a Kitchen Consultant, subtracting the day-care expenses, and how much sales would be required to match my full-time salary. It was risky because at the time, I had never earned more than $350 a month doing Kitchen Shows. Walking away from a job with a weekly paycheck and benefits is not an easy thing to do."

During the evenings when Michael was able to stay at home with the baby, Julie presented Kitchen Shows; within nine months, her Pampered Chef income surpassed her earnings at her previous full-time job and she had become a Director.

"As I took this work seriously," she explains, "and treated it like a business, I was able to build a team. Isn't this what successful people do in all professions? They go to college, take continuing education courses, read trade journals, meet regularly with their peers, and so on. Well, this is how I approached this business. I attended conference workshops conducted by the company's top performers, I checked out videos and audiocassettes from the Pampered Chef video lending library, I scrupulously read all the newsletters and other literature that the company distributes, and I was in regular contact with other Directors, picking their brains, learning from their experiences. Likewise, I made sure I did a minimum of two shows a week in order to hone and improve my craft. Of course, the fact that I enjoy what I'm doing so much made it easy for me to do all of this."

Julie's professional approach paid off. In 2003 she was recognized as one of the four people in the company who qualified in five Pampered Chef categories: personal sales, personal recruiting, first-line cluster sales, balanced business, and developing Directors.

Educated and trained in the youth ministry field, Julie began her working life with a job serving young people and families, guiding them to grow spiritually. She was consumed with a passion to serve people, and it has been her life's mission since. "Before I could give up such a meaningful career and replace it with a Pampered Chef career," she says, "I had to come to terms with myself. Could I sell food choppers and have the same job satisfaction? Well, I discovered that I'm still working with families, building mealtime traditions. *The Pampered Chef is not about the food chopper!* It's about teaching people the importance of family mealtime. I'm still serving people. The company's mission statement clearly defines what this company is about. What we really do is provide an avenue for families to connect at the dinner table."

Julie also points out that as a Senior Director, she contributes to her downline Consultants by helping them succeed in a career that provides them flexible hours to spend more time with their families.

"It has been particularly rewarding to me," Julie concludes, "to have been able to start in an area that was not aware of The Pampered Chef, and to see my team and I have such a positive impact on the entire community."

CHANDRA PANNELL

Chandra Pannell, who became a Consultant in 1996, is currently an Advanced Director. She lives in Ohio with her husband and two children.

While enrolled as an accounting major at the University of Akron, Chandra worked in a co-op program interning in the audit department at the world's largest rubber manufacturing company, Goodyear Tire & Rubber Company. Upon her graduation in 1989 at age twenty-three, she accepted a position in the Akron area with Goodyear. Later that summer, while Chandra visited her older sister in Chicago, the two young women attended a craft show where a Pampered Chef Consultant had set up a display.

"My sister was familiar with the company's products," Chandra says. " 'You've got to check out this vegetable peeler!' she raved. 'It's the best I've ever used.' My sister was married and was into cooking. Being single, I was never in the kitchen. I had never heard of The Pampered Chef. When I went back to Ohio, I settled in at my dream job with Goodyear, got married, and we had a son and a daughter. I was a working mom, and I forgot about that day at the craft show in Chicago with my sister."

Seven years later, in October 1996, a co-worker of Chandra's handed her a Pampered Chef catalog. "I'm hosting a Kitchen Show!" she exclaimed. Chandra remembered it was the same company that made that vegetable peeler her sister had raved about. "Now that I was cooking for my family of four, I ordered one," Chandra says. She looked at the name on the back of the catalog—Linda Chesmar—and called her to book a show. "Two years previously, we had moved into a new neighborhood, and I had met only a handful of my neighbors. I figured this was a good way to get to know them. Sure enough, a dozen women came to my show. The products Linda talked about in the starter's kit included many I wanted. Linda mentioned that signing up as a consultant was as easy as giving four Kitchen Shows. *Okay*, I thought to myself, *that's fair enough. It sounds easy and I'll also make a few extra dollars.* I had absolutely no interest in pursuing anything beyond those four shows. I liked my job as an auditor at Goodyear, and with two small children at home I had little time to spare.

"One of my co-workers hosted my first show. Getting up in front of fifteen of my peers was a bit intimidating, especially in front of people I worked with who knew me as an auditor. I felt uncomfortable and kept thinking that this is something I'd never do again. But when that first show was over, I had decent sales and everyone loved the products. I even received a few compliments about how well I did. I went on to my second show, and it went even better than my first. I also got some bookings and made some money. By the time I did my first four shows, I had committed myself to do future bookings, and had to follow up on them. I guess you could say I got involved because I didn't know how to get out of it."

By the end of that January 1997, she had done seven successful shows. "In January the company gave double points for our sales production to motivate everyone to start the year off with a bang. I had nearly seven thousand points toward an incentive trip to Hawaii, a twelve-month contest that required sixty thousand points to qualify. My strong start really excited my husband Eric, thinking of the free trip to Hawaii.

" 'You know, honey,' Eric said to me, 'if you really made up your mind, not only will you qualify for the trip to Hawaii, but you could build a business where you could manage your own team and quit your job at Goodyear.'

"I took that goal to heart, and started to book shows regularly while also recruiting people for my cluster. If I could build a team, I could build a business that would allow me to walk away from my auditing job. When Eric and I figured out the expenses we'd eliminate—our day-care bill, gas to work, dry-cleaning expenses, and so on—I realized that even if I only came *close* to matching my Goodyear paycheck, I would be ahead of

the game. Of course the biggest bonus didn't have a price tag—
the time that I'd be there for my kids.

"Eric was my biggest supporter. He kept putting signs all over
the house to remind me of my goal. I'd find notes on my refrigerator, bathroom mirror, and windshield. I was motivated. But
what really turned me on was a trip to Chicago in July 1997 to attend the National Conference. I loved hearing Doris speak about
The Pampered Chef's mission. And although I have read the mission many times, it was so much more meaningful hearing it coming from her. I especially enjoyed listening to her talk about
spending quality time with her family—with two small children,
I strongly identified with her message. She stressed that as consultants, we could help other families sit down at the table with
each other. This reinforced the added value I believe we provide
to our customers. By the time the Conference was over, I decided
this was something I wanted to do full time. I quit Goodyear in
December and that same month I was promoted to Director. It
was a bold move, because at the time, my Pampered Chef income
was nowhere near what I made at Goodyear. Walking away from
a steady paycheck was a little scary. It took a lot of faith, but I
knew God would provide me with a good business. I am blessed
to be surrounded by good people and a supportive husband."

The flexibility she has with her Pampered Chef career has
been a huge plus in spending time with her children. "My ten-
year-old daughter Lauren wasn't making the grades she was capable of in school," Chandra says. "So my husband and I agreed
that I should home-school her for six months. After I showed
how her schoolwork could be applied to real-life experiences, she
appreciated her studies more. To teach her fractions, I gave her
assignments such as calculating measurements for baking ingre-
dients. She was responsible for counting out mommy's money,
and I always trusted her numbers. When I made a bank deposit,

I wrote down whatever numbers she gave me on deposit slips. In a short time her self-confidence skyrocketed. Home-schooling Lauren was a growing experience for both of us, one I could not have attempted as an auditor at Goodyear.

"Most important, my daughter was able to observe my work habits," Chandra adds. "To succeed in this business, you must be a self-starter, and Lauren saw that no one had to tell Mommy to work. Now Lauren is a self-starter, and I'm so proud of her. She is now back in school and doing very well. My business slowed down a bit during the period I home-schooled Lauren, but it was worth it. If I had to, I'd do the same thing again for her or for my son Evan. I consider myself very fortunate to have a career where I have the option to make the choice." Today, Chandra has surpassed her income at Goodyear; she has over two hundred people in her sales organization, and she is proud of the fact that she operates a thriving business.

As an African American woman, Chandra believes that some minority groups shy away from business opportunities because of their fear of discrimination. "It's a culture thing," she says, "and this sort of barrier takes time to overcome. A Pampered Chef career makes it easy to start your own business because you have a formula for success clearly spelled out for you. You don't have to reinvent the wheel. And there is no limit on how far a minority or any other person can go in this business. The Pampered Chef is a true equal-opportunity company. Every Consultant starts out with the same sales kit, and how far he or she advances is strictly determined by merit.

"And I also like the fact that everyone abides by the same rules. For instance, one month my sales totaled $3,999.68. I was thirty-two cents short of four thousand dollars. Had my sales exceeded four thousand dollars for the month, I would have received some free products, valued at fifty dollars. I was short, I didn't get them. I was disappointed, but I liked knowing that the company treated me the same as it treats every other Consultant. On occasion I tell others my story of coming up thirty-two cents short, so everyone in my cluster knows that the company does not make exceptions for anyone. Everyone receives that exact treatment, no matter who he or she is."

CAROL RADU

Carol Radu is a National Senior Executive Director living in Texas. After receiving a degree in German at the State University of New York, Carol worked for Lufthansa German Airlines in New York City. In 1988, her husband was transferred to Texas. At the time, their son Peter was two years old and Carol was expecting a second child. Relocated in Texas, Carol quit her job to become a full-time mother.

In May of 1991, Carol was invited to a Kitchen Show at a neighbor's. "My good friend Paula and I belonged to the same Bible study and playgroup, so I felt obligated to go," Carol says. "Growing up on Long Island, I had always looked down on home parties. I suppose I had that cynical New York attitude toward direct selling. But since Paula was having all of our mutual friends over—the people I was closest with since coming to Texas—I went along with the crowd. In retrospect, I might have had a small glimmer of interest because I enjoyed cooking and I loved to entertain. I was intrigued by the Pampered Chef concept that offered exceptional kitchen tools not readily available in retail stores.

"During the presentation, I sat on a big sofa between my two neighbors. Each of them kept saying to me, 'Carol, you should do this. This is right up your alley.' Everyone was having a good time.

"Toward the end of the show, the Consultant asked if anyone was interested in being a host. 'Carol, if you don't feel comfortable having a show,' Paula whispered in my ear, 'I'll host one for you at my house. I really think this is something you should do.'

"I thought about it for a month. At least once a week, Paula called to say 'Come on, Carol, let's go.' A month later I hosted a show at my house. Afterward, I signed up to be a Consultant and did my first show at Paula's house.

"My real motivation was that my husband traveled all the time," Carol says, "and with two small children, I didn't get out of the house much when he was gone. Some of his trips were extensive—five weeks in Japan were not uncommon. I'd literally hand the kids off to him when he came in the door so I could 'escape.' I'd go to the mall and walk around for a few hours, trying to regain some sanity. I needed the change in scenery for the sake of the family, because if Mama ain't happy, ain't nobody happy. It wasn't possible to be in a mall for that long and not spend some money. Sometimes I spent a lot of money. But going from two full-time jobs with good salaries to a one-income family put a damper on my shopping sprees. With my Pampered Chef career, I could be out with people, and instead of spending money, I was making money."

Carol's two friends were right—she was a natural in this business, personable, articulate, and enthusiastic. Her Pampered Chef career took off from the very start.

"When people ask me, 'What motivates you now, Carol?' my stock answer is, 'I do this business to create a lifestyle for my family.' With all due respect to the business, I view it as a means to an end. And that end is my family.

"I look at my two children as a gift from God," Carol continues. "Someday He is going to ask me, 'I gave you two incredible gifts. What did you do with them?' I want to be able to look

Him square in the face and say, 'I have always considered them precious gifts from You, and I always did the best that I could for them.' "

To Carol and her husband, doing the best for their children includes providing them with good educations. Both children are enrolled in parochial schools with strong academic curricula. Her son Peter, now in his senior year, is a 4.0 GPA student and a standout athlete. But to Carol, education goes beyond the classroom. The Radus have traveled to Europe many times in what Carol describes as a wonderful cultural experience for all. The family also has a regular season subscription to the Symphony. "We want the children to have an all-around education."

With Carol's earnings, her husband Gheorghe cut back on his travel schedule to spend more time at home with the family. While the decision didn't affect his income, it did curtail future opportunities for advancement.

"I strongly believe that mothers should have the option to stay at home with their children," Carol emphasizes. "There is nothing that can replace Mom or Dad being home with the kids. This is what a Pampered Chef career provides, and making this opportunity available to other families is what I find so rewarding. It's what drives me today.

"Just the other night, I asked my daughter Katie if there is anything she learned from growing up in this business. She said, 'Oh yes! The most important lesson I learned was that first you work and then you play. And you don't get to play until you've worked.' Then she added, 'When you play, it feels so good to play because you've worked hard and earned it.' "

NANCY JO RYAN

Nancy Jo Ryan is a National Senior Executive Director living in the Greater Chicago area. When she joined The Pampered Chef in September 1986, she was one of only sixty-three Kitchen Consultants. Today she heads the company's largest sales organization, a business with annual sales in the $25 million range.

The mother of two young children, Nancy Jo Ryan had retired from an accounting career to be a stay-at-home mother. Her youngest child Richie was seriously ill his first year of life and the family incurred substantial medical bills. To earn some extra money for her children's Christmas presents, Nancy Jo was looking for a direct-sales position. A friend told her about a Pampered Chef Kitchen Show. "It was the best evening I ever spent away from my family," her friend told her.

"I was really intrigued," Nancy Jo recalls. "My friend gave me the name of her friend. Two weeks later the woman got back to me with a name to call. When I called the Consultant, instead of inviting me to a Kitchen Show, she came to my house with a crate of products and talked about the Pampered Chef opportunity. I was looking for some extra money to buy Christmas presents for my children. That was my goal."

She picked up her starter kit and held a Kitchen Show that very night. With total sales of $197, Nancy Jo calculated that her take-home pay averaged slightly more than $10 an hour. "Ten dollars an hour was good pay, considering it was part-time work. More important, I was having fun. I loved that I didn't have to 'sell.' I believed I was sharing what could be done with the products, and then giving people the freedom not to buy. I'd tell everyone, 'I only want you to come and enjoy the food and the company of your friends. If you need something, wonderful, then let me help you equip your kitchen.' I was perfectly content to make some extra spending money for the next couple of months and *have fun*. I never applied any pressure on anyone. After all, I was an accountant—what did I know about selling? Meanwhile, I sure did have a lot of fun."

By the beginning of December, she had reached her goal. Her Pampered Chef money was more than enough to buy her Christmas presents. "As my husband said, 'Mission accomplished.' "

Nancy Jo so thoroughly enjoyed what she was doing, she got three to five additional bookings at every show. She kept a list of seventy-five women who had requested to host a Kitchen Show. "Because I planned to leave the business after Christmas, I was going to give these leads away to others in my cluster at the January meeting," she explains. "Then my husband said to me, 'Gosh, honey, you've got all this business sitting here. Are you sure you want to give it all away?'

"So I said, 'What would you say if I did this two nights a week?'

" 'Nancy Jo, that would be fine,' he answered. 'You could get so carried away with this, I know you could do it seven nights a week.'

"My husband knows that when I love something, I throw myself into it a hundred percent. We set parameters we felt would work for our family, and I was off and running. I got on the phone and booked two to three shows a week, knowing that there'd be some rescheduling; for the next four years, I averaged two shows a week. The secret to my early success was my consistency. I'm a disciplined person, and I stuck to my plan. By getting enough people to enough shows, I got enough sales and enough recruiting leads to build a business.

"There are three kinds of people who come into this business: the hobbyist, the part-timer, and the individual who wants to make this a full-time career. I always tell people, 'You hold the measuring stick. I can't want something more for you than you want for yourself. So, you tell me what you want, and I will do my best to help you get there. Of course, you have to do your part.'

"Once I decided to stay, I started to recruit. I thought, 'If this is working for me, why wouldn't it work for others?' I signed up five people as consultants in less than a month at the beginning of 1987.

"The secret to success in this business is, make what you do look easy," Nancy Jo says. "If a guest says, 'That was a great Kitchen Show, I could never do that,' then you're doing something wrong. You may like the pat on the back, but you won't recruit anyone that way. You want people in your audience to say, 'She's having fun. She's making money. And I think I could do it even *better* than she does.' "

With her positive approach to business, Nancy Jo has built a two-thousand-person sales organization and is one of seven recipients of The Pampered Chef's prestigious Legacy Award. She received this honor in 1993 for her outstanding leadership in recruiting. One of the first individuals to recognize her Pampered Chef career as a potential business, she blazed a path for others to follow.

"I believe I can impact the people I work with," Nancy Jo declares. "This is a unique situation, because I'm not a boss, nor is anyone an employee. In my role, I mentor people. It goes beyond a business relationship, because a lot of personal and family matters come up. I love the fact that the only way you can succeed in this business is by helping others succeed."

RANDY WEISS

A former nurse, Randy Weiss joined The Pampered Chef in 1987. She was one of three individuals in 2001 to be named National Senior Ex-

ecutive Director, the new highest level of leadership for the company's top achievers. She lives in Missouri.

A couple of weeks before my first extensive recruiting trip in 1987, Randy Weiss answered an ad placed in a suburban Missouri newspaper. "I had a B.S. degree in nursing and was actually looking for a nursing job," Randy recalls. "But I came across an ad that read, 'Do you enjoy cooking? Do you enjoy quality kitchen tools? Do you enjoy working with people?' I was intrigued. I called the Chicago phone number and chatted with a nice, polite woman at The Pampered Chef.

" 'You should meet Doris,' the woman said. 'She'll be in your area the first week of July. Let's set up an afternoon appointment so she can show you the actual kitchen tools.'

"I marked the time and date on my calendar. But after I hung up, I started having second thoughts. In explaining the company to my husband and friends, I told them, 'I guess it's something like Tupperware but with kitchen utensils.' Everyone said to me: 'Why don't you get a real job? You're trained in nursing.'

"I kept putting off canceling the appointment until it slipped my mind. Well, on July 3, I got a call from a woman who introduced herself as Doris Christopher. 'We were scheduled to meet at the hotel where I'm staying; I've been looking forward to meeting you,' Doris said. 'I'm disappointed that you didn't come.' She was so polite and soft-spoken, I felt badly for standing her up.

" 'I am so sorry!' I apologized, 'I meant to let you know that I don't think what you are offering is for me, but I just got busy.'

" 'You really should come to see me,' Doris said. 'You don't know what you're saying no to. Why don't you come and at least see the product line?'

" 'It's my daughter Emily's first birthday party today, and we have a house full of out-of-town family.'

" 'I'll tell you what,' Doris said, 'my husband and two daughters are flying in from Chicago tomorrow afternoon for the weekend, so I've got some time on my hands in the morning. If you can't come to the hotel, I'll come to your house in the morning.'

"I was surprised she was willing to see me the next day. Not only was it a Saturday, it was the Fourth of July. 'Okay,' I said reluctantly. 'If you don't mind my house being a mess, I don't mind either.'

"After I hung up, I kept thinking about what a bad time it was for her to visit me. Besides having a house filled with company, I had to clean the house. In addition, we had plans to go downtown later in the day to beat the crowd and get a good parking place to see the fireworks that night.

"The next morning, Doris promptly arrived at my front door, carrying a crate of kitchen tools. I was breastfeeding Emily at the time. 'My place is a mess, and I'm in the middle of—'

" 'That's okay, I have two daughters of my own, so don't mind me,' Doris said, and we got right down to business. She showed me a kid's pumpkin cutter, and then the vegetable peeler, all the while telling me why it was better than others. Then she took out a measuring cup that measures solids such as peanut butter, shortening, and so on. Meanwhile, I'm thinking how much I'd really like to have these things. Even as only an occasional cook, I was quite excited. My husband was at home, so I called out, 'Bill, I want you to meet this lady.' Before I knew it, he was more excited than I was. 'What a great idea! Randy, you've got to do this.'

" 'Where do we go from here?' I asked Doris.

" 'You should have a Kitchen Show at your house,' she said.

"A few days later, the UPS driver delivered a deep-dish baking stone from Doris. The note read: 'Enjoy using the stone. I will call you in a few days.' This was such a nice touch. I'm thinking, 'Nice lady. Nice company.' I felt that this is something

I had to do. Still, I was starting to get cold feet. We set up a show on a day when Doris would be in town, but without sufficient coaching on how to be a host, I did such a poor job setting it up that we had to reschedule it. When I finally had a show, eight people showed up, including my sister and mother. Throughout the show, they kept saying to each other, 'Why is Randy doing this? She's trained to be a nurse.' They were not the least bit discreet—everyone could hear them."

The show grossed only $200 in sales, but Randy booked three more shows. I could see she was disappointed, but I kept telling her that the show was a big success. "The important thing is to book future shows," I stressed. I could tell Randy was not completely convinced. "Look," I told her, "you got three bookings to get your business started. What a great start!"

In addition to becoming a Pampered Chef Consultant, Randy took a nursing job for a local school district, and also did some private-duty nursing. "It was the best of both worlds," she says. "Now I could work my schedule around my daughter and be a stay-at-home mom." For the next three years, Randy worked part time for The Pampered Chef. Her husband Bill's produce business was going through some difficult times, and her Pampered Chef income helped pick up the slack.

I believed Randy had wonderful natural leadership skills, and I encouraged her to recruit other women and build her cluster. In the beginning, I sensed she was apprehensive, and she didn't quite grasp why she should focus on building a sales organization. I kept telling her it would pay big dividends down the road.

"Then Doris came to visit with Nancy Jo Ryan, one of the top Directors who lived in Chicago," Randy says. "After the three of us met with my group, we went out to lunch and my husband Bill joined us. Back then, I was making about $7,000 a year and Nancy Jo was making $35,000. Once I realized what

Nancy Jo was building, I started to think that if she could do it, so could I. It didn't happen overnight, but eventually I realized I could make considerably more money in this business by building a sales organization. While making a hundred dollars or so a night is good and fine, a lot of follow-up and phone calls are required. But by making another three percent on what your first-line people sell, and one percent on the people *they* recruit, it starts to add up. I started to focus on recruiting, encouraging my people to bring five recruits on board so they could be Directors. As Directors, their earnings increase, they see success, and they're more likely to continue.

"This is not a get-rich-quick business. But it keeps building; my income grew exponentially. Year after year it would grow by twenty-five to thirty percent."

At a National Conference in 1991, Randy was recognized as the company's top recruiter, and was a featured speaker at the Conference, which back then was attended by about two hundred people. "I had just taken a full-time nursing job because we weren't making ends meet," Randy says. "But I got so pumped up at this Conference, I made the decision to quit nursing and do this full time. That way I could work my schedule around Emily and not have to put her in day care. At the podium, I was bursting with enthusiasm and excitement. Although I had a prepared speech, I ad-libbed and told everyone that on Monday morning I was going to walk into my employer's office to say, 'You can just keep this job—I'm outta here!' Once I said this in front of my peers, I had to do it. I just asked the audience not to mention it to my husband because I wanted to be the one to tell him. Bill, realizing how strongly I felt about it, gave me his full support."

What is Randy's secret for success? "You've just got to ask," she says matter-of-factly. "You'd be amazed at what you can get in life by just asking. For example, I'll ask for a better table in a restaurant; I can't tell you how many upgrades I've got on airplanes and in hotels. Why? Because I asked for it! I think the art of listening and asking questions is crucial in business. I ask people if they'd like to come into this business, because I think recruiting is the top priority. Then I ask them to host a show. After that I'll ask, 'What about doing a catalog show?' Next I'll ask, 'What about buying another product?' It never hurts to ask. I do it in a nonaggressive way that doesn't offend anyone."

Randy and I go back a long way. We've traveled around the world together on Pampered Chef trips and have become very close with each other's families. Randy and Bill attended my daughter Kelley's wedding this past year. The night before her wedding Kelley reminded me that in Puerto Vallarta, Mexico, "Randy taught me to barter, and I bought that pair of earrings. Do you remember, Mom?" I did. Randy has watched Julie and Kelley grow up, and I watched her two daughters, Emily and Kathryn, grow up.

We've been together in good times and in bad. At age fourteen, Randy and Bill's daughter Emily was stricken with ovarian cancer; after a valiant two-year fight, she developed a brain tumor and passed away. Emily had accompanied Randy to many Pampered Chef functions, and she was dearly loved by all of us. We mourned with the Weiss family and will always miss Emily.

Randy's eyes water when she says, "Our family went through a horrendous period. Although we're still not past our grief, Doris and The Pampered Chef people have been exceptionally supportive. Not once has anyone pushed or pressured me in my work. They let me do what I have to do to get past this. I don't think that would have happened in another line of work."

KATHY YELLETS

Kathy Yellets, Executive Director, lives in Oklahoma. After receiving an M.B.A., she sold business systems for Hewlett-Packard. She became a Kitchen Consultant in July 1994.

"My sister called me after attending a Kitchen Show," Kathy remembers. 'I went to a party where they used clay things to bake bread!' she exclaimed, referring to The Pampered Chef's stoneware. 'We had such a good time. I thought that this is so *you*, Kathy.'

"I got the name of the Consultant that my sister met, Penny. Although she lived ninety minutes away, she came to my house to do a show.

"After everyone left, I went upstairs to tell my husband Dean about it. 'I'd like to give this a try,' I said. 'I can start trying it out with my friends.'

" 'What's it going to cost?' he asked.

"I didn't know, but it wasn't important. 'This isn't anything like selling for Hewlett-Packard,' I explained. 'It's more like teaching. And like HP, it's about relationship selling. People buy from HP because of who we are, and the support we give. I already know that part of selling. I believe everything I've already been trained to do will work for me here.'

"Dean worked for HP too, and we both enjoyed great incomes. But I wasn't looking at this for the money. It was just a fun thing to do. I had no other fun things in my life. I had my work and my family, but I didn't belong to a book club. I didn't do a bowling league or bingo. There was nothing I did that let me get away for a few hours on a regular basis. I felt I needed this to fill a void in my life. Dean wasn't too keen at first. With a five-year-old daughter and three-year-old son, our evenings revolved around our children, when we bathed them and told them bedtime stories. But seeing how excited I was, he said, 'Go ahead if you really want to do it so badly. The kids and I are behind you.' Our agreement was that I would do one Kitchen Show a week."

Kathy also wanted to make a difference in people's lives. "I know of no other product line that releases women from feeling tied to that kitchen," she explains. "It's an albatross that so many women have around their necks, and I think we've put some passion into creating a meal and bringing people to the table. When I do a Kitchen Show, people learn techniques and pick up tips so they can prepare what I call signature meals. It makes a statement about the fact that you spent time thinking about them. It's like going into a Hallmark store and getting a special card for someone. It lets them know you care.

"The first time someone who attended my Kitchen Show told me how much it meant to her, I knew this was the work I wanted to do. I wasn't getting that satisfaction from selling HP systems. Once my husband realized this, he understood that this meant more to me than simply getting out of the house."

Once Kathy started putting more effort into her Pampered Chef career, she quickly became a Director, seven months later. At this point she began to see her Pampered Chef career as a unique business opportunity. Three years from her first Kitchen Show, Kathy was working for The Pampered Chef full time, and her Hewlett-Packard work became her part-time job. "Full-time here was only twenty to twenty-five hours a week," she says. "It was wonderful. I was working far fewer hours, making more money, and building a business for myself. And my family was thrilled because I was spending more time with them than before. My fifteen-year-old daughter and I have a standing lunch date every Wednesday. I pick her up during her lunch hour at school and the two of us go to a restaurant. When I was selling HP systems, this wouldn't have been possible."

As a full-time Director, Kathy applied her business school education to build her business. "Done right, this job requires the same set of skills as running a small business. Your hands are in every aspect of the business. There is no manager telling you what direction to go in. If you don't get up to go to work on any particular day, you've lost a day of business. If you don't invest in it wisely, you don't get return on your investment. It's an ideal career move for a business school graduate who's looking for experience running a business.

"What makes it so special," Kathy continues, "is that the company has kept the start-up costs low, so anyone can enter the business. And unlike other businesses that sell retail, including some other direct-sales companies, there is no inventory to carry. And the company ships everything to the host, so I never have to make deliveries."

Kathy has recently "hired" her thirteen-year-old son Sam as an office assistant. With his computer skills he helps her with correspondence and bookkeeping, and on occasion accompanies her to Kitchen Shows. "To Sam this is a social thing. We talked about it the other night on the way home from a show. He said, 'I know it's something you set on your calendar, and you have a responsibility to do it, but it just doesn't seem like work, Mom, because you enjoy it so much.'

"When he said that," Kathy says, "I thought, what a wonderful legacy to pass down to a child. I hope he always thinks of work as something to be enjoyed. And my children are learning another valuable lesson. Although my hours are flexible, they are not optional. I tell them, 'You can have flexibility in your life, but the work is not optional, it has to be done.' And they see this every day, because I'm there in our home happily doing my job. It's a great way to teach them a good work ethic."

9

THE BEST IS YET TO COME

We've come a long way since my first Kitchen Show in 1980. I remember that rainy night on my way to Ruth Niehaus's house, and how I deliberated pulling over to find a phone booth so I could call to cancel the show. Thank goodness cell phones weren't commercially available back then; had I had one, would I have made that call?

Thinking about all that has happened over the years is mind-boggling. However, we were always so busy and immersed in change that we took it for granted. It never overwhelmed us. Jay often says, "Go with the flow," and that's what we did.

We live in a constantly changing world, and in business you must anticipate change—your survival depends on it.

In a passage in Lewis Carroll's *Through the Looking Glass,* the Red Queen cautions Alice, "Now, *here,* you see, it takes all the running you can do, to keep in the same place. If you want to get somewhere else, you must run at least twice as fast as that." Although Carroll wrote his classic in 1872, the Red Queen's advice is still amazingly appropriate in our present fast-paced, highly competitive world, because today, standing still is the same as moving backward. You can be assured that if you don't go forward, others will pass you up. Take a look at what has happened in technology. Thirty-eight years after the radio came out, it had 50 million listeners. It took only thirteen years after television came out before it had 50 million viewers. And it took four years for the Internet to hit the 50 million mark. In 1999 there were 92 million users, up 50 percent from the previous year. By the time this book is published, there will be an estimated 200 million Internet users in the United States and Canada.

Technological change is occurring at an exponential rate that dwarfs all change in the past. With this in mind, no viable company can remain at a standstill. A business enterprise either goes forward or goes backward. Nonetheless, too many people have a don't-upset-the-applecart mentality. They are content with the status quo and resist the need to do things in a different way. They oppose change out of fear. They do nothing rather than risk making an incorrect decision. The irony is that refusing to accept change is also a decision—and usually the wrong one.

Great companies withstand the test of time by adapting to change. American Express, founded in the 1840s, was originally the Pony Express. It wasn't until 1891 that the first American Express traveler's check was issued, and the company didn't enter the credit card business until 1958. A company called the Computing-Tabulating-Recording Company that manufactured butcher scales and cheese slicers was founded in 1911. Tom Watson, Sr., joined the company in 1914. In 1924 the firm was renamed International Business Machines. Now called IBM, the company first moved into the computer world in the 1940s, when it developed the automatic-sequence controlled calculator, a machine that was over fifty feet long, eight feet high, and weighed almost five tons. Although it took less than a second to solve an addition problem, it took six seconds for multiplication and twice as long for division—considerably slower than today's five-dollar pocket calculator. Not until the late 1940s was the selective-sequence electronic calculator introduced, followed in the 1950s by the first large computer based on the vacuum tube. By 1959 transistors began to replace vacuum tubes. IBM continued to survive and thrive by adapting to change.

A common denominator of a great company is its ability to adapt to change. Study and you'll observe that *nearly everything* about a company is subject to change, including its name. When Avon Products was founded, it was called the California Perfume Company. A British brewing company changed its name after more than two hundred years from Bass to Six Continents—to reflect the fact that its brewery enterprise produced less than one-fifth of its revenues, versus its hotels, restaurants, and pubs. A more recently founded company, Palm, Inc., a maker of hand-held computers, changed its name to palmOne.

Locations and buildings change as well, as do products and people. While our name has remained the same, the Pampered Chef logo has changed. We also changed buildings as well as locations. Our products have changed as we constantly improve them and add new products to our existing line. We introduced more than thirty new products at our July 2004 National Conference, a record high.

At Princeton, a student challenged his professor, Albert Einstein. "Why are you giving last year's test?" he asked.

The brilliant scientist replied, "Because this year, the answers are different."

In other words, what worked in the past may no longer be relevant. I believe all great companies share great product innovation. It's not enough to offer the same goods and services year after year. A company must keep improving; it must stay relevant.

But one thing about a company that should never be subject to change is its principles. As Thomas Jefferson said, "In matters of principle, stand like a rock; in matters of taste, swim with the current." We live by these words at The Pampered Chef. While we are quick to embrace change, we never compromise our values and principles. It is in fact, our mission:

> We are committed to providing opportunities for individuals to develop their God-given talents and skills to their fullest potential for the benefit of themselves, their families, our customers, and the company. We are dedicated to enhancing the quality of family life by providing quality kitchen products, supported by service and information for our Consultants and customers.

This is what we stand for. We purposely narrowed the statement of our mission down to two sentences so it can be quoted verbatim, and most importantly, practiced in our actions. With so many other aspects of the business changing, both internally and externally, The Pampered Chef's commitment to our mission remains rock solid. We are committed to enhancing the quality of family life. That was my intent when I gave my first Kitchen Show, to teach people easier and better ways to prepare food for their families and provide them with the kitchen tools to do it. While the process has been refined and improved over the years, our basic commitment remains intact. To this day, everything we do revolves around the Kitchen Show. It's been this way for a quarter of a century, and the Kitchen Show will continue to be the focal point of this company going forward. We believe it separates us from other companies. Our well-trained and well-informed Kitchen Consultants make a difference in people's lives.

And through their efforts—via thousands of Kitchen Shows every day—we bring families together at mealtime.

The family unit has been and remains the nucleus of our society. People will always eat meals at home, and this involves preparing food in the kitchen, passing down family recipes, and being together. These things are not going to change; I believe this bodes well for our company.

To quote Warren Buffett: "If past history was all there was to the game, the richest people would be librarians." When he buys a company, he never interferes with its management—he wisely gives them complete autonomy, knowing that they have more expertise in running the company than he has. Interestingly, Warren Buffett has never sold a company that he purchased in its entirety. (One of his many famous quotes is "Our favorite holding period is forever.") He is the ultimate long-term investor. This says a lot, considering he has purchased more than sixty companies during his unparalleled career.

We didn't want to sell to someone who would flip the company in a few years to make a quick profit. That would be disruptive to our sales organization. Our prime objective for selling the company was our desire to do what is right for the people who have been loyal to us.

We shared the same philosophy as Warren Buffett about the importance of valuing one's reputation. He once said, "We can afford to lose money—even a lot of money. We cannot afford to lose reputation—even a shred of reputation. Let's be sure that everything we do in business can be reported on the front page of a national newspaper in an article written by an unfriendly but intelligent reporter. In many areas, our results have benefited from our reputation, and we don't want to do anything that in any way can tarnish it."

During our first conversation in Omaha, he said to me,

"Doris, it's only fair to tell you that you will be no richer after the sale than now."

He looked me squarely in the eye and explained: "The ownership of your business already makes you wealthy and soundly invested. A sale would change the form of your wealth, but it wouldn't change its amount. If you sell, you will have exchanged a one-hundred-percent-owned valuable asset that you understand for another valuable asset—cash—that will probably be invested in small pieces (stocks) of other businesses that you understand less well. There is often a sound reason to sell, but if the transaction between us is a fair one, the reason is not that you, the seller, can become wealthier.

"Obviously, no matter what I pay you for your business," he continued, "if you just held it and ran the company the same as you have been running it, you would amass considerably more over the years from retained earnings, because it is a very profitable enterprise."

Jay and I were aware that because The Pampered Chef was indeed profitable, it would be worth far more in ten years.

"Why, then, do you want to sell it?" he asked.

"What we are looking to do," I explained, "is ensure the future of our business by making sure that it doesn't unduly depend upon one individual or one family. We are concerned about the consequences if something happened to my husband and me, leaving the company in a state of limbo. We want to make sure, for the sake of our seventy thousand sales representatives and one thousand employees, whose livelihood depends upon the continued success of the company, that it would be in the hands of strong leadership and on a sound financial basis. We want to be assured that the culture of the company, along with our philosophy and mission, remains intact."

He nodded. I continued, "I don't want to sound entirely selfless, because obviously if something happened abruptly, our heirs would have a problem deciding who would run the company, and we want to protect their interests. But yes, it would be easier to just keep on doing what we're doing."

This conversation occurred during the early stages of our initial conversations. He was trying to figure out what was motivating us to sell the company. I realized how much Warren Buffett values honesty, and that he is very good at sizing up people. At our first meeting, he wanted to get everything out on the table. Why are we doing this? Was there some skeleton in the closet? Was there a health issue? Because he and I both knew the company would likely increase in value, he had to understand financially why it made sense for us to sell.

"We like to do business with someone who loves his company, not just the money that a sale will bring, although we certainly understand why he likes that as well," he said to me. "When an emotional attachment exists, it signals that important 'qualities and values' are likely to be found throughout the business—honest accounting, pride of product, respect for customers, and a loyal group of associates having a strong sense of direction."

"I agree," I replied. "And I believe that what you say is an accurate description of The Pampered Chef."

Two years have passed since we were acquired by Berkshire Hathaway. Today, we know we definitely made the right choice.

The success of The Pampered Chef could not have happened without the help of many others. The people here at our home office and 70,000 field people share my belief that they can make a difference in people's lives. How well they understand that the table is the place of refuge in an often-troubled world. It is at the table that we keep close to our family and friends. The table is where we share good times and times of trouble, sorrow, or concern. And it's at the table where we can share a meal and spark a dream in the heart of a child. It is also the place of giving, as you invite people into your home. Such giving teaches our children about sharing and hospitality. At The Pampered Chef, we provide people with ways to be creative in the kitchen by giving them simple, fast ideas and the tools to accomplish them. I believe that as long as our people adhere to the company's values and remain dedicated to serving others, good things will continue to happen at The Pampered Chef.

I'm reminded of our family reunions every summer in Michigan when I was a little girl. At a potluck dinner, there was always a bountiful array of food displayed on a long table, including platters of delicious baked chicken, ham, roast beef, potato salad, homegrown vegetables, and homemade breads. At the end of the main course my mother would announce, "Well, I hope you left some room for dessert. We've got homemade pies—apple, cherry, blueberry, and peach. And there's lots of fresh fruit, cakes, cookies, and homemade ice cream. So hold on to your forks, everyone, the best is yet to come."

Every year, I looked forward to our family reunion because each one always seemed even better than the previous year's.

I often overhear some of our Consultants saying the same thing at our annual Pampered Chef Conference. Someone will say, "This Conference is better than last year's." Inevitably, someone else will add, "How are they going to be able to top this one next year?" Yet interestingly enough, I've heard the same comments at each succeeding Conference.

So to paraphrase my mother, we at The Pampered Chef have a lot on our plate. And *the best is yet to come!*

ACKNOWLEDGMENTS

My heartfelt thanks go out to all the people who helped make this book a reality. I'd like to thank my literary agent, Al Zuckerman of Writers' House, who believed in our project from the beginning. Robert Shook, our writer, worked with me so closely helping me to recall and capture all the moments in time that, collectively, became the chapters and pages in this book. Thank you, Bob, for your sensitivity, your work ethic, and your way with words. At Doubleday, we had the world's best editor, Roger Scholl, who brought forth the essence of all we wanted to say in the most eloquent way possible. Thank you, Roger, for your keen eye and commitment to the written word. Also at Doubleday, Sarah Rainone, assistant editor; Michael Palgon, deputy publisher of Doubleday Broadway; Meredith McGinnis, associate director of marketing; David Drake, director of publicity for Broadway and Currency Doubleday; Laura Pillar, senior publicist; Janelle Moburg, VP and sales liaison; and the Random House sales force.

At The Pampered Chef, I would like to thank our president, Marla Gottschalk, whose strength, leadership, and commitment will allow our company to continue on its path of excellence, ethics, and growth. I also thank the leader of our parent company, Warren Buffett, chairman of Berkshire Hathaway, whose belief in The Pampered Chef is unwavering. Jane Edwards, our global public relations officer, has spearheaded this project from beginning to end with the able help of her corporate communications team led by Lisa McComb.

I also want to thank the Kitchen Consultants who shared their personal stories in this book. They were selected by the editorial team at Doubleday to represent all of our thousands of Kitchen Consultants. It is truly our Kitchen Consultants and our Home Office Co-workers who deserve the greatest thanks of all. You have built a company that is truly beloved by millions.